Advance Praise for 𝓠

"Tara's book delivers a necessary and inspiring message to all women today. She writes with authority, courage, and profound insight. This is a perfect woman-to-woman gift."

— Caroline Myss, *New York Times* bestselling author of *Anatomy of the Spirit* and *Sacred Contracts*

"Reading *Sexy + Soul-full* was a revelation for me. At once, Robinson both names and dismantles the damaging messages we internalize about what it means to be a successful and productive woman. And then she offers a new perspective and tools for reframing our beliefs and habits so that we might live with more ease and equanimity. This book is my new guide for presence, productivity, and living from the heart."

— Lisa Congdon, artist and author of *Art, Inc.: The Essential Guide for Building Your Career as an Artist*

"Tara brings a uniquely feminine approach to productivity, one that chooses authenticity over perfection and open-heartedness over control. Her gentle approach to getting things done will help women find greater freedom to do what they love."

— Susan Piver, *New York Times* best-selling author of *Start Here Now: An Open-hearted Guide to the Path and Practice of Meditation*

"In *Sexy + Soul-full: A Woman's Guide to Productivity,* Tara Rodden Robinson makes a compelling case for making time for what matters and what you love joyfully and unapologetically. She also charts a step-by-step roadmap for getting things done the gentle, mindful way through defining what success means to YOU as opposed to the competitive, masculine approach to productivity. Tara's book is a much needed antidote especially for women who do too much. It's not a strict formula but a feminine perspective on productivity and a soulful guide enriched with her touching story. After reading Tara's book, my perspective on productivity and time management shifted totally. I don't think I can ever look at myself, my life, and my to-do list quite the same way again."

— Cigdem Kobu, writer and entrepreneur, founder of
PeacefulTriumphs.com

"Women everywhere: Read this book. Tara uses her own story as a platform for describing a process that — wonder of wonders — shows us how to live a fully expressed, love-filled life. Productivity for women is, and needs to be, different than is conventionally understood, and Tara not only gets that, she gives permission to be vulnerable and real while becoming our true selves in the very best way possible."

— Karen Wright, Executive Coach and author of *The Complete Executive: The 10-Step System for Great Leadership Performance*

"A remarkable, honest narrative from which I learned many new things. Rich in surprises and insights."

— Rose Caiola, Founder and CEO of ReWireMe.com

Sexy + Soul-full

ALSO BY TARA RODDEN ROBINSON, PH.D.

Genetics for Dummies

40-Days Forward: Your Journey to a Life of Abundance and Meaning

Sexy + Soul-full

A WOMAN'S GUIDE TO PRODUCTIVITY

TARA RODDEN ROBINSON, PH.D.

SAINT MICHAEL'S PRESS

A SAINT MICHAEL'S PRESS BOOK
4 WEEMS LANE, NO 133
WINCHESTER, VA 22601

stmichaelspress.com

Cover artwork by Tara Rodden Robinson, Ph.D.
Layout by Veronica El-Showk
Cover Design by Silvina de Brum

ISBN 978-0-9964726-2-3 (softcover)
ISBN 978-0-9964726-3-0 (electronic version)

PRINTED IN THE UNITED STATES OF AMERICA

To Mama,

for her love and unfailing support.

TABLE OF CONTENTS

PREFACE

I t took me almost two years to complete the writing of this book. My journey started in earnest thanks to a conversation with my husband, Douglas. Spring had arrived but, like most years in Corvallis, Oregon, the weather was still rainy, gray, and chilly on that May morning of 2013. He'd taken me to our own bit of Paris, a small pastry shop a few blocks from our home, to enjoy a buttery-rich, cream-filled, almond croissant and a hot, smoky French Roast coffee.

As I picked at the last crumbs of my pastry, I started whining about an acquaintance of mine. "His book is trite! He doesn't have anything original to say! And he's sold over 25,000 copies of the damn thing. I just don't get it," I said, fuming. The truth was, I was jealous of both my colleague's notoriety and his checkbook. In spite of the hours spent healing my soul, with the help of a pastoral counselor, and working my tush off to release my insane desire to enjoy some form of celebrity as a productivity guru, I still wanted to be well-known and sought after for my expertise. Ok, and to be admired and liked, too.

My ever-patient husband listened to my diatribe and gazed at me with love in his eyes. He said, "Everything you want will come to you when you finish writing your book."

I sat back, stunned into silence.

Douglas had been encouraging me to write my book for years but I'd always been deaf to his coaxing. This time, however, it was as if he'd just performed a miracle that had given me back my hearing. When we got home, I rushed to find some paper. I made a dozen little signs, all with the same message: *Everything you want will come to you when you finish the book.* I posted them everywhere—the bathroom, my closet, my office, my art studio, even in the gratitude journal that I write in every night before I go to sleep. That sentence was practically the first thing I saw every morning and the last thing I looked at before turning out the light every night, every single day, for the next eighteen months. What I didn't know was how writing *Sexy + Soul-full: A Woman's Guide to Productivity* would change me or what the process would demand from me.

Writing this book taught me so much about myself, where my loves come from—those things my soul desires to be happy—and how the thread of these loves has kept me on course, even when I felt entirely and completely lost. I gained unexpected insights and grace from understanding "enough," the joy in ease, and the power of equanimity. I ended up forging an entirely new perspective on success and I was able to articulate what years of failure and disappointment had gifted to me. And the changes were more than internal.

My mode of dress became more flowing and artistic. My sense of self was more centered and affectionate. I felt sexier and certainly more soul-full than I felt at the beginning of my writing journey.

But the journey was not all sweetness and light. I also encountered tremendous self-doubt.

About halfway through producing the first draft of the book, I entered a period of deep discouragement and desolation. I lost hope in my ability to finish, and became mired in worries. I feared I had nothing of value to share with my readers. But, I used every practice in this book and I kept myself going. Through prayer and with encouragement from my friends and family, I became convinced that completing my book was a matter of immense personal and spiritual significance.

It was an imperative that I had to finish, come what may. Not because I would get "everything I want" but because to have abandoned the effort would have been a crime. By refusing to deny myself of the gift of completing the book, I came to recognize that success is, and always has been, entirely up to me.

When I began writing, I was longing for fame or a monetary reward that would serve as a sign that I'd arrived at "Destination: Success." The journey started because I was envious of what another writer had accomplished. I wanted what he had—or so I thought. That's what my little signs pointed to: "Everything you want will come to you..." But honestly, I had no idea why I was called to write the book nor what would come when I finished the manuscript.

The turning point came from a conversation with my dear friend, Augusto Pinaud. I was bemoaning my lack of success—not just in writing the book but more generally. He gave me a journal prompt: *What would "successful-Tara" tell "today-Tara" about how she became successful?*

Using that question as a beginning, a single journaling session yielded one of the biggest aha moments of my adult life: My success isn't about my income or how well known I am. My success is something that I determine; it comes from inside me. Success is also something already inherent in me. All I needed to do was lay claim to it. From that insight, I gained the confidence to resume writing and to complete the manuscript.

In the book, I take the risk of sharing with you who I really am. I value authenticity and vulnerability very highly. That's part of why I include my own story as part of the guide. It seems to me that appearing perfect at any cost is important, even essential, to many experts. I understand. Professionally, I feel pressured to look as if I have it all figured out, too. Frankly, perfect isn't real and perfect isn't relatable, which is why I'm sharing my journey with great honesty.

All of us struggle, and I'm no exception to that. I have ups and downs, weaknesses and flaws, strengths and gifts. I have failed many times over and I expect that as long as I'm alive, I'll go on experiencing failure with great regularity. I am willing to share my short-comings and difficulties with you because I want you to know that you're not alone. And furthermore, if I've overcome my struggles, that means you can, too.

Last, but not least, I share my story because I've made a lot of mistakes over the years. I abandoned my loves, became deaf to my own inner wisdom, and swallowed other people's definitions of success. Working through those mistakes consumed a lot of time and energy. By letting you see where I went wrong, I might be able to save you some heartache and speed you toward owning your success a lot sooner than I embraced mine.

An important take away message from *Sexy + Soul-full: A Woman's Guide to Productivity* is that love is the pinnacle of success. When you commit to making time for what you love, unapologetically and joyfully, everything changes. Your perspective shifts. What was impossible becomes possible.

I also want to invite you to adopt something I know to be true: You are already successful. No degree, no paycheck, no promotion, or accomplishment on your resume is needed. Success is not a designation or a character trait. Success is something inside you that you own. When we, as women, fully claim and own our success without squirming or hiding, we can change the world. I am sure of it. May it be so.

INTRODUCTION

Before I began exploring the world of productivity, my own life was a mess. I constantly struggled to complete the simplest tasks, like remembering to eat or making sure I'd had a shower recently, because most of my attention was devoted to getting my academic career off the ground. Like many aspiring researchers, my default answer to every question put to me was 'yes.' Yes, I'll develop that new course on a topic I know very little about. Yes, I'll collaborate on an area of research that's way outside my area of expertise. Yes, I'll apply for another grant, write three manuscripts, and review a dozen proposals...today.

I kept oodles of complex projects going at once, including a multinational research program, and that wasn't the half of it. In the evenings, I took music lessons from a Celtic fiddler, while teaching myself to paint with pastels on the weekends. In addition, I was a wife to a wonderful man, himself a professor, and I was a loving daughter to my aging parents.

Naturally, in the midst of all this frenzied doing, I overlooked important details. Helpful and important emails went unread and unanswered at such a rate that it still boggles me. I lost track of necessary communications, for example, the message from a colleague about analyzing our jointly collected data set. By the time I noticed she wanted me to work with her to publish our findings, she'd pulled in someone else to help her, and they went on to publish the paper more-or-less without me. I was so furious that I stopped speaking to her, even though I knew deep down that I was to blame.

This was just one of the relationships that floundered on the rocks of my overwhelmed life. I often stopped working on one research project to work on another, and would then forget the left-behind item for months, even years.

Of all the important deadlines I missed during my decade-plus binge of overwhelm, the most significant was I forgot to have kids! By the time I finally got around to rectifying that critical oversight, I was 38. My doctor's suggestion that I start medication immediately to stimulate ovulation left me completely mystified. I was healthy and at the top of my game. Drugs were for women who had problems conceiving, not overachievers like me! Oddly, my confidence was barely shaken by the three years of trying, and I finally got pregnant at age 41.

Although at this time in my life many of the days went by in a "fast-forward" blur, the end of my all-too-short pregnancy stands out with immense clarity. I distinctly remember the terrified look on the technician's face as she searched vainly for fetal heart tones and the sorrowful expression my doctor wore when she told me that my baby was dead. With a broken heart, I sobbed as I drove away from the clinic and, literally, went straight back to my office. I buried my grief under my busyness where I mummified my sadness under more layers of endless doing.

Rather than taking time to grieve the loss of what turned out to be my one-and-only chance at motherhood, I started making an effort to gain control over my workload. I found a slim volume entitled *Getting Things Done*, sporting a cover with a picture of a friendly-looking man named David Allen. Allen emphasizes keeping lists and tracking all the action items that arrive from emails, meetings, and bright ideas. To manage of all of your work, he advises creating a "trusted system" consisting of tending a calendar, making to-do lists broken up by categories like "email" or "errands," and carefully labeling and alphabetizing complex filing systems.

Allen's methodology, also known as GTD, inspires a sort-of cultish obsession with software, technology, and tools, and I soon sought out fellow practitioners with whom to talk shop. At first, I found the method itself overwhelming because by actually writing down everything I was doing, I saw, for the first time, how insanely overloaded I was. But soon, my sense of control increased, and I felt calmer. Over time, I even became a recognized expert in GTD, and for seven years, I hosted a twice-monthly podcast that drew thousands of listeners from across the globe.

At midlife, women naturally begin to ask themselves "What do I want?" and place much greater importance on realizing, or at least pursuing, their own deepest inclinations.

Like most productivity approaches, GTD is aimed at helping you get more done so you can take on still more. The unspoken ethic is one of competition: Be better than the other guy to get ahead. This dogma correlates nicely with traits of masculinity such as primacy of work (putting work ahead of everything else), winning, and pursuit of status.

But by the time I became a sweaty mess due to my first barrage of hot flashes, I was sick of attempting to conform to these masculine attributes of productivity. I was no longer in academia, and I found myself longing for a more feminine approach to work. Although I could handle more tasks and check off more to-do's, I realized that all I was doing was cramming in more of the same.

My teacher and mentor-from-afar became Dr. Christiane Northrup. I turned to her book, *The Wisdom of Menopause: Creating Emotional and Physical Health During the Change*, for guidance. Dr. Northrup helped me recognize and understand that my life's priorities were evolving and unfolding naturally, in synch with the changes in my hormonal and physiological states.

"Our culture expects women to put others first," writes Dr. Northrup, "and all during the childbearing years most of us do, no matter the cost to ourselves. But at midlife we get the chance to make changes, to create lives that fit who we are—or, more accurately, who we have become."

All the sacrifices I'd made for my career, including putting work first and motherhood last, came into view in a very new, harsh light. As I entered the end of my "childbearing years," my new insights also explained why I was feeling so darn restless and hungry for new possibilities. Northrup explained that at midlife, women naturally begin to ask themselves: "What do I want?" and place much greater importance on realizing, or at least pursuing, their own deepest inclinations.

Throughout my academic career, I'd wrestled with feelings that I was a complete impostor. Even with my constant doing, I couldn't get shut of the notion that I was barely one step ahead of being exposed as a massive fraud and a complete failure. No amount of accomplishment or achievement mollified my sense that I was never, ever, going to be successful.

Practicing GTD exacerbated my lack of confidence partly because of its emphasis on capturing every single idea and inspiration without regard to the fact that there was only so much of me to go around. Worse still, Allen emphasized getting desired outcomes as the definition of success. Paradoxically, however, when I *stopped* defining success as achieving my desired results, I often experienced greater happiness and welcomed all of my outcomes—both the anticipated and the unexpected—with much greater joy and equanimity.

As I began to realize that my success was not entirely correlated with obtaining my preferred results, my perspective on productivity began to shift. I embraced contribution—bringing my gifts to the world and giving them freely and generously—with less concern about how my gifts were received or what happened to those contributions after they were made. By letting go of accomplishment as the measure of my success, my desire to compulsively seek more to do and to fill my every waking moment with scheduled activities diminished. The drive to constantly achieve was replaced with a deep desire to create, nurture, and savor.

I also stopped viewing time as my enemy. Instead, I came to experience an incredible freedom from the clock, and with that freedom, a growing confidence that I could realize my most closely-held

...ions and dreams. That's how *Sexy + Soul-full: A Woman's Guide* .. *roductivity* was conceived.

What Makes This Book Unique?

My book is intended to provide you with a feminine perspective on productivity. For too long, women have been hammered with the notion that they can (and should) "have it all." This cultural imperative is predicated on two equally damaging falsehoods: "You are not enough," and "More is always better." Both of these white lies encourage women to over-commit, to say "yes" to everything, to pit having a family against having a career, all while telling women to define their worth by their accomplishments. Simultaneously, the work world, which is dominated by men, harps on putting our families and our loves last—or at least, putting them aside—in favor of career achievement and work success.

While women are caught between trying to have it all and putting their loves on hold, the productivity experts pile on their primarily masculine values and viewpoints, giving women no truly feminine and heartfelt guidance on how to "get it all done" and still have energy, joy, and stamina to enjoy their lives.

Sexy + Soul-full productivity is not about "having it all." It's about having enough.

Sexy + Soul-full productivity is not about sacrificing your loves on the altar of your career. It's about putting your loves first, unapologetically, and placing your work in support of those loves.

Don't get me wrong. I'm interested in helping you with being productive at work. I'm just not interested in using that productivity as a justification for doing more while pushing your loves aside. Instead, I'm dedicated to helping you with productivity so that you can have more being. More being creative. More being still. More being joyful. More being spiritual. More being with the people you love in the places you adore. More being you!

Sexy + Soul-full: A Woman's Guide to Productivity is aimed at helping you define productivity on your own, fully-feminine terms. To realize that productivity, you need certain skills in managing the demands you face to make time, space, and other resources available for being creative, passionate, artistic, spontaneous, generous, and whatever it is that your heart is calling for you to *be*.

WHY SEXY + SOUL-FULL?

When I started writing this book, and my friends asked me what the title was, I'd smile and tell them (at first, a little self-consciously). More often than not, they would go wide-eyed and exclaim, "That sounds amazing!" Those joyful pronouncements were often followed by questions for more details. "What do you mean by Sexy + Soul-full?" I know it may sound provocative, but I didn't title the book merely to garner attention, although saying "Sexy" and "Soul-full" in the same sentence with "Productivity" is fun. No, I chose Sexy + Soul-full as descriptors for some really important reasons.

Not only is the productivity field steeped in masculine values, but the approaches focus on the intellect, ignoring anything that happens below the neck. I find this particularly ironic in light of a print advertisement I ran across recently. The ad features a photo of a professional man, depicted as an architect or builder, with a caption that reads, "When something needs to be done, you make it happen." At first glance, I figured the ad was for another productivity book or some kind of task management software. But no. They're selling a famous blue pill that enhances erections. What the ad implies is that intercourse is just another work project, devoid of intimacy, romance, or emotion. This kind of productivity is obviously neither sexy nor soul-full. Erectile dysfunction aside, physical considerations profoundly impact productivity.

For instance, walking for just forty minutes three times a week improves cognitive functions, including decision-making, planning, and prioritizing—all essential skills for work productivity. Other studies show that regular aerobic activity calms the body, making stress less damaging, improving learning and retention of new knowledge, and boosting mood as much as antidepressant medications. In fact, getting just four hours of cardio a week can erase the effects of burnout and stave off depression entirely. Thus, acknowledging and incorporating the physical is imperative to your productivity practice. Fortunately, we women are uniquely well-suited to recognize the mind-body connection.

Maybe it's our monthly cycles or childbearing that keeps us rooted in our bodies. Not that men can't have a firm grasp of the interplay between mind and body, too, but women seem to be much more in tune with how our bodies and minds interact (in my experience). This intuitive understanding of the mind-body connection brings up another aspect of our lives that other productivity methods ignore: the life of the spirit.

Women tend to be much more holistic with respect to integrating our spiritual selves into our lives. We are aware of body, mind, *and* spirit—and this is reflected in our intuition and our senses when making

When a woman is truly sexy, she is confident, bold, centered.

plans, interpreting events, and creating meaning for ourselves. We are much more likely to consult our heart's inclinations than to take some more "rational," analytical way of making a decision, for example. And we're more comfortable in saying so, as well. To my knowledge, this heart guidance system has never been part of any productivity method or approach—until now.

WHAT IF LOVE WAS YOUR HIGHEST PRIORITY?

The Sexy + Soul-full approach is centered on what and who you love. You make those loves your number one priorities by *beginning* your planning around them—not by adding them on as an afterthought. When you make love your highest priority, it is very, very sexy. You can sense this reality immediately when you encounter a Sexy + Soul-full woman: She radiates a special presence that is both heavenly and profoundly down to earth, all at once. You may know her as your yoga teacher or you may see her in your favorite coffee shop; you may bump into her at an art festival or glimpse her running along a forested path. And when you see this Sexy + Soul-full woman, you recognize her.

Think about it. When a woman is truly sexy, she is confident, bold, centered. She exemplifies an incredible balance between investing in the intimate roles of life, while nurturing a healthy interest in the wider world. And nurturing is a key word for us women: We are, many of us, deeply nurturing. We are creative, relational beings who want to help in every way we can. That desire springs, in part, from our femininity. It's in our DNA. And when we're in our wheelhouse of womanhood, really standing in that truth, we are incredibly productive! We do what we love with vivaciousness. We infuse our work with lively energy. If this kind of productivity isn't incredibly sexy and soul-full, I don't know what is!

The physical and spiritual aren't two separate realms. Rather, they're intimately connected, and both part of Sexy + Soul-full Productivity. I truly believe that your body is a temple: a holy space that houses your sacred soul. The life of the spirit is essential—essential to living a full, joyous, abundant, and deeply-engaged life. No matter what your belief system might be, I am convinced that following a spiritual path is the key to discovering and living a life of passion, rich with meaning and ripe with significance.

The life of the spirit, as I experience it, is embodied—that is, it's experienced in my physical self as well as my mind. "For those who have eyes to see and ears to hear, our bodies offer us a continuous stream of invitations to awaken. This is why body awareness forms the foundation of all awareness. You can be no more aware of anything than you are of your body," writes David Benner.

When I feel love for the divine, I really feel it, in my chest. When I pray or meditate, I take on physical postures or movements that help me to communicate with God—in supplication, sorrow, joy, or listening. When I practice yoga, take a long walk, or immerse myself in physical activity, I gain greater access to my spiritual side at the same time. I think of my body as a genuine temple of the Holy Spirit, a home, a dwelling place, albeit a temporary one. Thus, the physical and the life of the soul are joined for me, and work together.

I believe having integrity across all the domains of life is incredibly important. By having integrity I mean being the same person no matter what context you find yourself in. This kind of authenticity is achieved when heart, head, and hands all agree. Put another way, when your mind, body, and spirit are all on the same page, you do everything with greater effectiveness. This is another reason why I emphasize expressing your soul-full self as part of being a productive woman.

Throughout *Sexy + Soul-full: A Woman's Guide to Productivity*, you'll be invited to explore with your spirit and to seek out new ways of experiencing a Soul-full lifestyle. I take an inclusive approach to this exploration because I want to welcome you no matter where you are in your spiritual journey. It's my hope that you'll be open to exploring the mystical and take a chance on encountering the divine as you read this book.

Are You Ready to Explore Your Path to Sexy + Soul-full?

This book is divided into three parts.

In Part I, you'll retrace your life's journey on a treasure hunt to (re)discover what you love. I'll share my own story, including how I developed, lost, and rediscovered my loves along the way. In telling you where I've been and how I got there, my intention is to help you connect with those parts of you that may have been forgotten or misplaced somehow. Our lives as women are often complicated and our paths are crooked. Many times, my own wandering path seemed to make no sense, and I worried that I'd never arrive at my destination and, even worse, I often had no idea where I was going! But, unbeknownst to me, my loves were with me all along. You'll have an opportunity to learn how your own loves have accompanied you, too, in the first three chapters of the book.

Part II examines the three destructive myths about time. These lies stand between you and your loves, making time into your enemy. To put these destructive myths aside, you'll be invited to undertake three apprenticeships: to enough, to ease, and to equanimity. When completed, these three apprenticeships will leave you firmly rooted in your ability to make time for your loves and any other activities that you want to make a part of your Sexy + Soul-full life.

Finally, in Part III, you'll put love into action. First, you'll be invited to undertake a process of discernment to set your direction. The discernment process is intended to provide a clarity in the efforts you'll expend in service of your loves. Because you have to start where you are and work with the trajectory your life already has, I provide a process for creating a heart-centered plan for moving toward your intended direction.

Your ability to achieve your aspirations is largely dependent on your capacity to make and keep promises to yourself. You can explore the joy of completion, how to set and keep intentions, and the potential of accountability. In the final chapter of Part III, I talk about the realities of results—and how to receive all your results with grace, no matter how delightful or difficult those results might prove to be.

Part I

(Re)Discovering What You Love

Owning our story and loving ourselves through that process is the bravest thing we will ever do.

—Brené Brown

Before you begin making time for what you love, you need to know what your loves are. Can you name what you love? What are your passions? What sets your heart on fire? At various times in my life, I've found these questions embarrassingly difficult to answer.

Losing touch with what you love is so easy. Crazy, huh? You'd think your loves would be the most important thing and that you'd be able to keep them firmly in mind. But the exact opposite is often the case. You get assailed by so many demands, so much to keep track of! And in a flash, what you love has been lost in the shuffle. Buried under years of toil, details, adversity, making a living, stress, emotional eating, grief, dust bunnies, and—yes—neglect. You wake up one morning, look in the mirror, and think "Who is that?!?" You don't even recognize yourself. At the same time, what you love may seem distant, out of reach, concealed, or nonexistent.

I've lost touch with my loves, too—more than once. The losses and (re)discoveries of my loves have taught me many valuable lessons about embracing and inhabiting a Sexy + Soul-full way of being. By exploring my past, I've seen how the divine accompanied me throughout my journey. In seeking out my loves and learning where and how I misplaced them, I've discovered that what seemed lost was actually the very thing sustaining me in my darkest and most difficult hours.

In this section, you'll be invited to go on a treasure hunt along with me. I'll take you on a journey through my own past. In each period of life, instead of looking for gold and jewels, I'll invite you to recollect your loves along with me and seek out clues to what your heart is longing for now.

Owning my story was frightening and challenging, but also empowering. By taking ownership of my story, I ferreted out sources of strength that I didn't know I had and I drew lessons about my loves that supplied me with great power for living my Sexy + Soul-full life. I hope you'll find that owning your story will give you many great gifts, too.

Perhaps you are certain of exactly what you love and are ready to get started making more time for it. Even so, I encourage you to explore your story, unearth your past, and seek the hidden jewels waiting for you there.

chapter one

The Archaeology of the Soul

Like archaeologists of the soul, we need to excavate our hidden
depths to unearth the shards of the spirit, and then reassemble those
fragments into a whole self.

—Caroline Myss

The seeds of our loves may have been planted when we were girls, and that's the first place we're going to explore in our journey to rediscovery. Unlike true archaeologists, who dig through layers from the most recent into the distant past, we'll explore our lives starting from the beginning.

When Wonder and Shame Collide

On the buffet in my living room, you'll find my favorite photo of myself as a little girl. I couldn't have been more than five or six at the time. I've got a pixie haircut and I'm outdoors. In the background is the little wooded lot that was next to our home in Louisiana. I'm not smiling.

Instead, I've got a fierce look on my face and my hands are raised in the imitation of a lion's claws. Gazing at her picture now, I have so much love for that little girl who was so lively and energetic. In looking at other childhood photos, I see the first tender roots of much that is part of me now. In the velvet dresses I wore to church, I see the beginnings of my spiritual life. The girl on the horse reminds me of my thirst for outdoor adventures.

What's missing from these photos is other children; I was an only child with no brothers and sisters to keep me company. At home, I was lonely; at school, I was the outcast kid. My life as an outcast began in fourth grade. The year before, 1968, my parents had enrolled me in private school. The move was in response to a Federal court order in 1967, which forced schools to desegregate. I know my mom and dad had my best interests at heart when they took me out of the public school system and sent me to River Oaks School where not a single person of color, other than the janitorial staff, could be found. Their reasoning was that I'd get a better education at River Oaks, and perhaps I did. One of the early lessons I learned was how cruel people can be.

One bright fall morning, I was gazing out the window of the cheap, dingy green, portable building that housed our classroom. A large soaring bird swooped past and my fourth grade teacher, Mrs. Lakeshore, heard my little gasp of delight. In a booming voice that got the entire class' attention, she inquired as to what I'd seen. With great enthusiasm, I shared my wonderment, "I thought I saw a chicken hawk."

"I tawt I taw a chicken hawk," she exclaimed with the same tone and delivery used by Tweety Bird from the Bugs Bunny cartoon when he says, "I tawt I taw a puddy tat!" The room erupted with laughter. From that moment on, I was an outcast. No one, not even my former best friend, would play with me at recess. I was mocked, ridiculed, teased, tormented, bullied, and rejected by my River Oaks peers for the next four years.

Mrs. Lakeshore taught my most vivid childhood lesson: What happens when wonder and shame collide. And this example brings up an important guidepost in your own search for your misplaced or lost loves. Many of our loves go into hiding because of a moment when shame, ridicule, or bullying frightened us into withdrawing from our awe-filled and authentic selves. We may be or become so ashamed, scared, or wounded, that we forget what our loves look like. Could we be face to face with a love and not recognize it? Yes. Absolutely. That's how powerful these kinds of shaming experiences can be—they can distort our understanding and blind us to our loves.

Like actual archaeological finds, the items we unearth from our pasts may be caked with gunk that hides their true identity and value. But beneath the dirt, lies a shard of your spirit, shining and waiting to be uncovered. While you are (re)discovering this treasure, you may also find the roots of other loves planted there as well. Amazingly, difficult experiences like these can provide fertile soil in which loves can thrive.

The seeds of my deep love of solitude and my fierce independence were sown during and after the fourth grade. I immersed myself in books and gained not only a deep love of reading, but also an incredible ability to concentrate and completely lose myself in the world the author has created. I spent hours reading, high in the backyard treehouse my dad built for me. In spite of Mrs. Lakeshore's taunting, my love and wonderment in the natural world is still a part of me. Even now, I feel

Many of our loves go into hiding because of a moment when shame, ridicule, or bullying frightened us into withdrawing from our awe-filled and authentic selves.

best when I'm connected to the outdoors and I still get giddy when I see a Red-tailed Hawk swooping down from the sky.

My mom planted, watered, and encouraged my spiritual roots. She took me to church every Sunday where, despite the hellfire and brimstone preaching that rained down from the pulpit of our Southern Baptist church, I gained an understanding that God loves me. I still remember my excitement and joy at the moment of my decision to go to the front of the church and to declare that I wanted to give my life to Christ. I was seven years old but I felt so new, as if I was seeing the world for the very first time. In the evangelical tradition that I grew up in, being "born again" is considered the path to redemption. That's precisely what it felt like to me in that moment. I felt like I'd just arrived on earth, new and clean and perfect and loved. Even though I would later lose my faith in God, twice actually, the vivid memory of that moment is still with me. However, practically from the beginning of my religious life, I thought I was supposed to be a Catholic.

I'm not exactly sure how I became convinced that I belonged in the Catholic church. Perhaps my attraction to Rosary beads, incense, and Italianate statues of saints came from Mrs. Slavant. My mom hired Mary Slavant to take care of me between the time school let out and when my parents got home from work. Mary, whom I always called

Mrs. Slavant, was a rotund, agreeable, Greek-Italian woman who spoke four languages: Greek, Italian, French, and English. She took me with her to Mass now and then and taught me how to say the Our Father. In contrast to the worship services at my home church, Mass was peace-filled, quiet, and predictably soothing. I loved kneeling in prayer and I particularly adored the Virgin Mary, whose statue, surrounded by flickering votives, seemed like an oasis of heaven on earth.

When I, a soul-full little girl, told my mom that I wanted to be a Catholic, she explained that being Catholic was "hereditary." In other words, people became Catholic by being born into Catholic families. Nevertheless, throughout my childhood and later as a teen, my love of all things Roman Catholic continued to grow.

Your spiritual upbringing is another rich source of memories to examine in your search for your loves. Even though your religious past may also include wounds or deep scars, your spiritual upbringing may still be one of your loves. Allow yourself to recall your experiences and look for times when you felt awe, wonder, or love. Maybe there was a moment when you felt a great sense of peace or comfort. Perhaps you simply knew or understood some wisdom that was beyond your years. Those can all be signs of your loves, as well as the tender touch of the divine.

My religious life wasn't entirely happy, however. Like so many aspects of my upbringing, church was one of the many points of contention between my parents. My dad didn't go to services with my mom and me. After his father died, my dad rejected religion, blaming God for his own father's death. Innocently, I once invited Daddy to come to church with us. He immediately started screaming at my mom,

"You did this! You put her up to it!" He reacted as if I'd asked him to rob a bank instead of attending a Sunday church service. I was desperate to stop him from berating my mom so I yelled, "Daddy, I did it because I love you!" Afterward, I remember sobbing uncontrollably. What I don't remember was if anybody came to comfort me.

My mom and I could never anticipate what would set my dad off. He would be calm one minute and yelling at the top of his lungs the next. As a side effect of my dad's frequent rages, I had nightmares. Not occasional sleep disturbances, I had screaming-bloody-murder nightmares, as regularly as clockwork, a couple of hours after bedtime. Every. Single. Night.

My mom tells me that I started having these night terrors when I was very small, about age three, and the nightly ritual of my screaming and her getting up to comfort me went on until I was eleven or twelve years old. What was I dreaming about? I have no idea. Even then, under my mom's intense questioning, I had no recollection of what invaded my sleep to cause my nightmares.

EXCAVATE THE DEPTHS

Despite—or perhaps because of—its wounds, your childhood is a rich treasure trove for you to mine, even if yours (like my own) was a childhood marked by times of misery. You had loves—many of them private and tender—and those loves can be of great help to you in rediscovering (or creating) your loves now. Take time now to recall your own younger years.

Excavate the depths by exploring your childhood:

- Find an early memory. Think about yourself as a child—as early as you can remember. What events stand out in your memory? If you have pictures of yourself as a baby or while you were in elementary school, bring those out. Who do you see in those sometimes faded and hazy photos? What did she love?

- Think of a time you felt shame. I know this may require some courage, but if you can bring yourself to recall your own moments of childhood shame, you may find one of your loves there, too. Consider a time when you felt delighted, experienced a sense of wonder, or were bowled over by awe, and then, for whatever reason, were shamed or ridiculed for it. Instead of focusing on the negative experience, turn your gaze to the wonder and look beneath the hurt. Describe the sacred shard that is hidden there.

- Create a collage or drawing to express the loves of your childhood. Whatever it is that captured your imagination as a little girl may speak again to your heart now. Collect images where you find them—from magazines, using Pinterest, or snapping photos with your phone. After you've gathered several, spend some time just gazing at them. Is there a pattern? Which loves speak to your heart from these formerly hidden depths?

Unearthing the Shards of the (Teen) Spirit

When you are growing up, is there a more fractured time than during your teens? This is when most of us start to explore all the "Me's" we might be. It's a *trying* time. Trying on identities. Trying out the boundaries. And trying our parents' patience. My teenage years were very, very trying for everybody involved.

When I was in the eighth grade, on the way to River Oaks one morning, I turned to my mom and said, "Next year, I want to go to public school." I was thirteen years old when I chose a different educational experience than the one my parents had selected for me. This choice granted me freedom from the history of being an outcast kid—I forged new friendships and created a new identity for myself at Ouachita High School where, at long last, I felt like I fit in.

After I turned fourteen, I wasted no time in trying all sorts of ways to numb the sadness and anger that had simmered in my body throughout my childhood. I sampled cigarettes, marijuana, and a few other substances, then settled on alcohol as my drug of choice. I understand now that getting drunk was not just a rebellious action on my part, but also a way to escape. Soon other means of escape became available to me, too: For my fifteenth birthday, my parents gave me a car. What were they thinking?!

> *All of the "shards of your spirit" are important to the process of exploring your inner depths and piecing together a greater wholeness now.*

When I saw that burnt orange, Oldsmobile Starfire, for the very first time, I burst into tears of joy. What the car represented to my parents, I don't know, but to me, that car was freedom. I spent hours on the road. From my hometown of Monroe, Louisiana, I would drive seventy-odd miles to Vicksburg, Mississippi, just to watch the massive Mississippi River flow past or to wander the Civil War battlegrounds. I'd park near the Ouachita River and sit for hours, alone, deep in thought. And on Sundays, I'd cruise Monroe's Forsythe Park, flirting with boys, gabbing with my friends, and listening to music.

I relished my independence, reveled in exploring historical sites, and indulged my vivid imagination by writing. My childhood spent immersed in books paid off. It was during these teen years that I discovered how to verbalize emotions in writing—both poetry and fiction—and began journaling as a form of expressing my deepest thoughts and emotions. I tried on other creative outlets, too, like photography and drawing. The ongoing role of nature in soothing my emotions or inspiring my creativity was deepened and shaped by those many hours spent exploring the wilds of Ouachita Parish, climbing over fences, and forcing long rusted gates to photograph century-old tombstones in overgrown cemeteries.

Being able to drive also meant the freedom to express myself spiritually, too. I didn't know I could choose to become Catholic but I did discover that most Catholic churches were unlocked every day. I spent hours in the darkened sanctuary of Our Lady of Fatima in Monroe, kneeling at the feet of the statue of the Blessed Mother, lighting candles, and praying. Often, I asked for refuge from the continuing battles between my parents or for the love and affection of whatever boy I was interested in at the time. It was during those times of prayer that my soul-full self developed from a child to a young woman: contemplative, thoughtful, and deeply attracted to the sacred feminine embodied in the Virgin Mary.

When I look back on my sometimes troubled teens, I see how so many of my life-long loves came to be. I was obsessed with rock music and loved singing along to my favorite records, using a hairbrush as a microphone. I spent my allowance on the latest releases by Heart, Lynyrd Skynyrd, The Doobie Brothers, Aerosmith, Boston, and Led Zeppelin—all played at top volume on the turntable in my bedroom. I spent hours sketching from the photos on the album covers, and my drawings illustrated the image of my ideal man: tall, slender, with long dark hair and a beard. As it turned out, my teenage self had great taste— my second husband bears a remarkable resemblance to the rockstars I was attracted to back then.

Of course, not all of the loves I acquired during this rite of passage were worthy of me, and some contributed to shattering aspects of my fragile sense of self. I binge-drank and I think it's safe to say that I loved getting drunk. I used alcohol as a way to numb the discomfort of being an awkward, lonely teen. I also loved attention in ways that were decidedly unhealthy. I sought affection from any boy who showed the slightest interest in me. While I wasn't promiscuous (my straitlaced Southern Baptist upbringing kept my knees firmly glued together), I gave my heart away all too easily, only to have it broken time and time again.

Experimenting and trying on different ways of being to see which suited us was a natural process in our teens. We may have tried on various personalities, modes of dress, and genres of music. Some of those styles fit us well, and others we discarded. During high school, the pressure to conform is often intense, and we may have tried on masks—ways of disguising ourselves and our loves in order to fit in. Keep in mind that while you were spreading your wings, you may also have been contorting yourself to conform to a shape that was not your own. Alternatively, some of those same masks may actually be expressions of a secret self, one you've lost track of as the years have gone by.

UNEARTH THE SHARDS OF YOUR SPIRIT

As you unearth the shards of your spirit, give your teen-self ample freedom to open her heart to you. If your teen years were anything like mine, you may have gotten very adept at keeping secrets, holding your loves as close as possible to your chest in an attempt to both keep them for yourself and keep them from being destroyed by others. You may have sampled many possibilities and loved them all. Conversely, your teens may have marked a time when love was a barbed object that left you wounded, scarred, and scared. All of these "shards of your spirit" are important to the process of exploring your inner depths and piecing together a greater wholeness now. Unearth the shards of your (teen) spirit:

- What did you try on as a teen? The nascent moments of freedom during your teen years are good places to seek out your loves. While your teenage pursuits may seem fragmented, when you look back these bits and pieces can be used to form a mosaic of sorts that can give insight into your teen spirit. Try rearranging these shards—the various personas and interests you tried on as a teen—and see what sort of picture emerges.

• What did you find yourself resisting or rejecting? During our teen years, we often find ourselves rebelling against the choices our parents made for us. What loves emerged from your exercise of free will?

Burying the Fragments of the Whole Self

When you go off to college, things begin to change. The craziness of your teens is put aside (that is, if you intend to graduate!), and finding a path that leads to making a living gets more emphasis.

I graduated from high school when I was only seventeen—not because I was a stellar student but because my November birthday had allowed me to start first grade at a younger age than most of my classmates. When I started applying to colleges, I didn't realize that my verbal score on the ACT (a standardized test intended to assess readiness for college) was only a few points short of perfect. Instead, I took the rejections from University of Texas and Ole Miss as evidence that I wasn't very smart. As a result, I ended up staying in my hometown and attending Northeast Louisiana University. I moved into a dorm on campus and took my first wobbly steps toward adulthood.

While some of the pressures to conform, like those many of us experienced in high school, become irrelevant when we get to college, often other sources of pressure emerge. For example, the practicality of needing to make a living when we graduate can squash our youthful idealism. Like the shaming experiences of childhood, the fears, hopes, or expectations of others may cloud our vision and obscure our loves at this highly impressionable time. When I started college, my chosen major was English but my dad, God rest his soul, was certain that I couldn't make a living as a writer. He fretted and worried and cajoled and frowned. Eventually, he began to extol the virtues of a more practical career: nursing. I so wanted to please him, to make him happy. Back then, I couldn't have known that I was incapable of making my dad happy. Making him happy wasn't my job, but I didn't learn this truth until much, much later. So I put aside my dream of being a writer and went to nursing school instead.

By acquiescing to my father's fears—that I couldn't make a living as a writer—I started to accept his fear as true. I allowed my dad's anxiety to become a lens, which blurred my vision of the future.

When I took my first tentative steps away from a writing career, I began misplacing, hiding, and stuffing away my true identity as a creative, artistic, and intellectual woman. For years, I'd taken a book with me everywhere I went and read during every free moment. As I was waiting for a class to begin one day, a young man named Gary saw me in the hallway and asked his friend, "Hey, who's the space cadet?" The friend introduced us, and Gary asked me out.

Looking back, I should have taken his jibe as the insult that it was and steered clear, but somehow his odd charisma attracted me to him. As he alternated between humiliating and wooing me, I molded myself into the person he wanted me to be. Gary was also a rabid atheist and hostile toward all spiritual expression. Under his influence, I lost my religious faith, stopped writing, and gave up on art. Worse still, I married him.

Shortly after we arrived at our new home, newlyweds in a new state, where he was attending graduate school, I stood in the parking lot of our apartment building frozen stiff with the stark realization that I'd made a terrible mistake. I didn't want to spend the rest of my life with this man—who, as it turned out, was not only addicted to pornography but also to manipulation, lying, and infidelity. In addition, Gary had something in common with my father: He was prone to fits of anger for ridiculous or petty reasons.

Not only was my soul-full self a casualty of my first marriage, but my development as a sexy woman came to a jolting stop as well. Gary emotionally and sexually abused me for almost nine years until I gained the maturity and courage required to leave him. During my teens, I'd discovered a feminine identity that included my style of dress, the jewelry I favored, and how I wore my hair. The beginnings of my confidence, expressed through my physical appearance, were the very aspects of my being that Gary ridiculed and suppressed. In high school and early college, I'd enjoyed wearing dresses and cute shoes. But during my marriage with Gary, my style of dress became boyish and shapeless. I was trying to recede into the background because I was so ashamed and embarrassed by who my husband was and how he treated me.

My desire to fade into the woodwork was particularly ironic because Gary placed an inordinate value on attention. I felt invisible during my childhood and teen years while my parents were occupied fighting. In our early courtship, when Gary showered me with attention, I abandoned my authentic self, mistakenly accepting his overtures as an equivalent for love. I became a pleaser and did whatever Gary wanted me to do so that he wouldn't abandon me as he sometimes threatened to do. Archaeological digs often turn up bones. In exploring your own life, you, too, may encounter skeletons. These remains may be frightening at first, and, perhaps, disgusting, too. But just as archaeologists gently and respectfully study the remains they unearth, you can also examine what you find with objectivity and compassion. You may see pieces of yourself that got buried, either by you or someone else, which you'd like to uncover again. Conversely, there may be memories that you'd like to leave interred. Either way, by excavating your hidden depths, you are likely to stumble across fragments of your youthful idealism, which is a by-product of loves you once treasured. These bits and pieces can be part of your whole self now, if you'd like them to be.

REASSEMBLE THE FRAGMENTS OF YOUR WHOLE SELF

Your story may be nothing at all like mine. Then again, you, too, may have had relationships with people who influenced you in unhealthy, and even deeply wounding, ways. No matter whether your scars run deep or are merely superficial, these kinds of life experiences can leave us in a state of numbness, especially if we have pushed our true selves down, far out of sight. We do this "stuffing" as a way to defend ourselves, and it's perfectly natural to hide those vulnerable parts of ourselves in an effort to protect our tender, most precious places. Now, you have the opportunity to restore those loves and use them as a means to guide yourself toward a whole, Sexy + Soul-full self.

To reassemble the fragments of your whole self, ask:

• Who might you have been if you'd stayed the course with your first loves? Not that the paths you chose as you began your journey from teen to adult were wrong, even if those choices led to painful lessons you wished you'd never learned. You are who you are now because of those experiences, and who you are now is precious, holy, and sacred. If your transition into adulthood was marked by a loss of your loves, you can still call those loves back out, into the light, after a long period of deep storage. Nonetheless, your interrupted paths may lead you back to early loves. Take some time to look back on what you might have done if left to your own devices.

• How did you express your sexuality as a teen? Most of us begin to explore our sexual identities during young adulthood. What did being sexy mean to you as a young woman, just out of high school? Our femininity is expressed in all sorts of ways. Might some of those aspects of your life give you clues to what your feminine loves were?

• What parts of yourself did you give up to please someone else? Many women give up parts of themselves to please other people. As you've seen in my own story, I gave up my developing identity as an intellectual, among other aspects of my authentic self. You, too, may have put away preferences, inclinations, and tastes, in an effort to be likable to someone else. Which of those would you like to reclaim for yourself now?

*You are who you are now
because of your experiences, and
who you are now is precious,
holy, and sacred.*

chapter two

The Doors to the World of the Soul-full Self

The doors to the world of the Wild [Self] are few but precious. If you have a deep scar, that is a door, if you have an old, old story, that is a door. If you love the sky and the water so much you almost cannot bear it, that is a door. If you yearn for a deeper life, a full life, a sane life, that is a door.

—CLARISSA PINKOLA ESTÉS

NEUROSCIENTISTS SAY THAT our brains don't fully mature until our mid-twenties. I believe I entered actual adulthood around age twenty-seven, when, in a very surprising way, I learned to stand on my own two feet. It was then when I began claiming my loves, pursing them with courage and boldness.

FINDING THE DOOR TO A SANE LIFE

After graduating from college, Gary and I returned to my Louisiana hometown. Early in my short career as a nurse, I found that I craved the intensity of high pressure work environments. Eventually, I found my way into the surgical department where I became a circulating nurse. A good circulating nurse is a master of process: She must learn not only the surgical procedures themselves but also the preferences and habits of the individual surgeons. The circulator does this to stay one or two steps ahead of the procedure, ready to instantly fulfill any request or need that arises. I found that I was brilliant at learning sequences of events and remembering them with exacting detail. My love of learning blossomed into a deep appreciation for, and expertise in, systems and processes.

At the same time, my heart began to yearn for something I couldn't name. I knew for certain that I was being called, but I had no idea what was calling to me. I only knew that my heart ached, and that the pain I felt wasn't entirely due to my abusive marriage. It seemed to me that I was supposed to be someone else. But who? To assuage my restlessness, I took up running.

I'd never been athletic in high school or college but I soon developed a disciplined running routine. Running helped me cope with the stresses of my work and gave me a perfect excuse to be outside. As I trotted past bayous and cotton fields, I became curious about the names of all the birds I was seeing. I bought a field guide and got hooked on bird watching.

How was I to know that this simple pastime represented a door to an entirely new life? As I identified warblers and swallows, flycatchers and egrets, herons and ducks, I could never have imagined that those feathered creatures were, perhaps, angels in disguise. As my knowledge of all things avian grew, so did my independence. Once again, just as I had as a teen, I roamed Ouachita Parish, enjoying both solitude and nature. Eventually, I joined the Louisiana Ornithological Society and, with my fellow birders, I explored scrubby woodlots all over my native state of Louisiana.

{A YEARNING, says Clarissa Pinkola Estés, can be a door to a sane life. The tricky part is that yearnings rarely make sense. We may find ourselves in the throes of a longing that is entirely out of sync with our status quo or our comfortable lifestyles. Sometimes, a yearning will express itself in dreams, as mine once did when I dreamt I was crawling around on the floor in an unfamiliar place, searching for something that I could not find or identify. I believe these yearnings are our loves, calling to us from their hiding places, expressing their own longing to be found. If we are willing to move toward them, even if somewhat tentatively, we will often find a door that leads to them.}

I discovered the door to a sane life, the identity of my yearning, in the spring of 1990. Almost from the beginning of my obsession with birding, I'd had a "thing" for the rainforest. Most of the migratory birds I searched for every spring spent their winters in the rainforests of Central and South America. These tropical regions are home to the majority of the world's biodiversity, and I wanted to see these places for myself. But that wasn't the whole of it. I loved the rainforest like a teenager loves a rockstar—in an obsessive, deeply emotional, totally irrational kind of way. When I went to Costa Rica on a birdwatching trip with a group of birders from Louisiana, it was as if I'd gotten my "backstage pass" to the big show. We traveled to a remote rainforest reserve and hotel called Rara Avis.

I believe yearnings are our loves, calling to us from their hiding places, expressing their own longing to be found.

Wandering around the jungle on my first day at Rara Avis was everything I'd ever imagined. At a forest pool, I watched as a hummingbird flew down to the water and delicately dipped its body into the water to bathe. The sounds of Howler Monkeys and the voices of hundreds of birds sounded a symphony of epic proportions. I gazed in wonder as blue, iridescent *Morpho* butterflies the size of saucers floated past.

When I met the owner of the hotel, Amos, he took one look at me and asked, "Are you a biologist?"

"No," I replied. Why would he say such a thing? I was wearing knee-high rubber boots (a necessity in a habitat that gets upward of two hundred inches of rainfall a year), khakis, and a long sleeved shirt to protect me from the mosquitoes. Around my neck, I was carrying a pair of binoculars. To my eye, I didn't look any different from any other birder in the group.

"Funny, you look like a biologist to me," he said.

I must have stared at him like he had two heads but Amos just smiled. All that day, I walked around with a marvel inside me. I felt that I'd heard the sound of my own name for the very first time. Could becoming a biologist be the answer to my yearning?

In the afternoon, Amos offered to take me for a ride on the cable car that researchers had built to access the tree tops where they conducted their investigations. We climbed into the small, open, metal cage. The floor space was tight, only about three square feet. Amos showed me how to put on my safety gear: a climbing harness with a carabiner to attach myself to the cage would prevent me from falling out of the cage if I lost my balance. Safety was important: The cable was strung over a deep crevasse, the edge of which was only a few feet from where the cage was perched. With a roar from the generator as it belched out a bluish cloud of smoke, the cage lifted off the ground and lurched forward, emerging from the exhaust-stink haze and immediately suspending us over a three hundred foot drop.

I felt no fear as the cage swung gently while we traveled along the length of the cable, grazing the tops of trees rooted at the bottom of the ravine almost five hundred feet below us. We passed over a river and then, as we moved into the blinding sunshine, Amos stopped the cage directly over a thundering waterfall. The deafening cascade, the sunlit water, and the warmth of the humid air assailed my senses. And in that moment my door to "the world of the wild Self" opened. I knew, with absolutely certainty and complete clarity, that I was going to live and work at Rara Avis.

That night, Amos and I sat on the front porch of his hotel and chatted. I told him about the longings I'd been having and my crazy love for the rainforest that seemed to make no sense. Finally, I shared my epiphany that happened over the waterfall that afternoon. After a long silence, he said, "Well, I guess I better give you a job."

When I departed Costa Rica and returned home, I cried for two weeks. The certainty I'd felt in the moment over the waterfall gave way to absolute terror. Finally, on a Saturday morning, sobbing in my bed, curtains drawn, completely miserable, the yearning inside me put its foot down and said, "Enough." I got up and dialed the phone. My heart was pounding and my hands shook, and not just because it was the first international phone call I'd ever made. When Amos answered, I blurted out, "When you said you'd give me a job, were you serious?"

The connection was crackly, his voice dim, and the delay agonizingly long. "Yes," he said.

My friends and family thought I'd lost my mind. I felt like I was jumping off a cliff. Even though I was terrified, I did what my heart and the deep yearning were calling me to do: I walked through the door to a fuller, saner, deeper life than the one I'd been living. I quit my job as a nurse, I left Gary, and bought a plane ticket. I didn't even speak Spanish but off I went to spend six months in the Costa Rican rainforest, where I became the resident naturalist at Rara Avis and learned to speak the languages of plants and birds and ecology.

When I returned to the States, I filed for a long-overdue divorce. Then I took the GRE and started applying to graduate schools. I was admitted to the University of Illinois, Urbana-Champaign, to study for my Ph.D. in Biology. Simultaneously, I decided that I wanted to believe in God again and I returned to the religion of my upbringing where I slowly regained my faith. My yearning had opened an unexpected door to an entirely new life. Little did I know that when I arrived in Illinois, yet another love was awaiting me.

SEEK THE MISSING PIECES

In the quote that opened the chapter, Estés tells us that the "doors to the wild Self are few but precious." I think of the "wild Self" and the Sexy + Soul-full self as one and the same. Our Sexy + Soul-full selves are the most essential parts of our womanhood, the most authentic, feminine aspects of our identities as individuals. During young adulthood, around that crucial age when our brains mature, many of us experience a strong sense that something must change. We know, deep down, that there is a missing piece in our lives, a sacred element we need to find in order to become whole. The doors to that wholeness can be many—a wound, a scar, a love, a yearning.

• As you look back to your young adulthood, you may discover a turning point that coincides with your late twenties. Return to that period of time in your memory. If you have journals, spend some time rereading your entries. Find photos and relive the scenes you see there. Recall to your mind any inclinations or yearnings that might have signaled a transition.

• What strange passions and quirky paths have called to you? My yearning spoke to me in unusual ways—through the voices of birds and the thundering roar of a waterfall. Make a list of the odd, whimsical, or out of the ordinary voices you've been hearing. Do these have anything in common with each other? What yearnings might be speaking to you?

• Longings can speak more directly through dreams. Try keeping a dream journal. Put a notebook by your bedside and before you arise, jot down anything you can remember about your dreams of the night before. Pay special attention to vivid dreams that include deep, rarely expressed emotions. After a few weeks, reread your notes and look for patterns. Do any longings or loves put in appearances in your dreams? Are there significant elements or themes like searching, grieving, finding, or loss?

SEEKING THE DOOR TO A FULLER LIFE

I was overjoyed to begin graduate school when I arrived in Champaign, Illinois. In some ways, being at a huge university was a dream come true. Vast knowledge was at my fingertips, and my love of learning could be unleashed at last. The downside was that almost as soon as my loves for birding, biology, and the rainforest had begun to emerge, I had to learn to protect the tender shoots.

Academia thrives on cut-you-down-to-size, soul-crushing, and vulnerability-punishing competition. Anything that didn't resemble the norms of the academic culture of the Department of Ecology, Ethology, and Evolution was subject to ruthless peer pressure, mocking, and ridicule. Come to think of it, graduate school had a lot in common with fourth grade. The torture included degrading my southern accent, which I started taking great pains to minimize. Amazingly, however, my spiritual life, which I'd begun to rediscover during my divorce, remained intact. I identified openly as a Christian—albeit practically the only one among my predominately atheistic colleagues.

As I struggled to make the adjustments needed to succeed, I tentatively approached one of my fellow students for help. I'd been watching him for a while by then. Tall and slender, with dark hair and gray eyes, Douglas was clearly very intelligent and, unlike others in our lab group, he wasn't attack-dog aggressive in intellectual matters. He kept to himself, and I took him to be somewhat shy and reserved.

One afternoon, I went down to Douglas' office and asked his advice on reading scholarly papers. I don't know why or how I summoned the courage to approach him because doing so required me to reveal that I didn't know how to glean understanding from the complexities of the literature. But ask him I did, and he was kind to me. A small friendship was kindled. A few conversations later, I started asking him out after lab group meetings. We'd go to the local watering hole, and he'd politely drink a beer with me—I learned later that he actually doesn't like beer—and we'd chat. Slowly, I realized that I was attracted to this gentle, sensitive young man. When we fell in love, we kept our relationship a secret, fearing that our colleagues would harass us. But eventually, our love for each other became impossible to hide, and a little over a year later, we were married.

Academia challenged my ability to be open-hearted, but I gained some new loves and strengthened others. I learned, for instance, that I had a talent for teaching. I loved revealing the inner workings of ecology to my students. I felt such joy and fulfillment when students would suddenly grasp a complicated concept or when they'd gain confidence with subjects that they'd previously found too daunting or difficult.

The deep independent streak I'd cultivated since childhood turned out to be to my advantage when Douglas and I ended up in Panama, literally hacking our way through the rainforest to establish a study site for our graduate research projects. My love of nature was magnified and encouraged as I conducted my field work and studied social behavior in Song Wrens, a sociable and melodious rainforest bird species. I acquired a deeper love of and appreciation for hard work during those years, as well. Douglas nurtured and encouraged my growth; he believed in me and affirmed time and again that I was capable, intelligent, and talented, not to mention, Sexy and Soul-full.

While my time in Panama was very good for me in many ways, the isolation from any kind of spiritual community that I could be part of left me vulnerable to discouragement. When my friend Lisa became sick with cancer, I prayed fervently for her healing. After she died, I threw a temper tantrum with God. I cried with such force that I became physically sick. And in my rage, I told God that I wasn't going to ask for anything ever again. However, the longing to pray wouldn't leave me. I found a copy of the Hail Mary and memorized it. I clung to memorized Catholic prayers—the Our Father, the Salve Regina, and the Hail Mary—as my little threads of hope for the next four years.

Just because you follow your loves, it doesn't mean you are going to the land of "happily ever after." The path you choose may still be rocky, and if you encounter obstacles, you may be quick to question whether you've made the wrong choice. I found much of my graduate school to be sheer torture yet somehow, I always remained convinced I was on the right path. The greatest lessons of graduate school were that I could endure failures and keep going. I acquired an inner stubborn streak along with a strong work ethic. However, my perspective did undergo subtle changes as I was fully enculturated in academia. I was never as competitive, career-focused and harshly critical as some of my colleagues were but, at times, I could certainly give as good as I got.

Eventually, we earned our Ph.D.'s, and Douglas became a professor at Auburn University in Alabama. We bought a house and got a dog. Finally, our lives seemed stable enough to consider having a family. Even though I had a solid foundation in biology, I didn't really grasp how age affects a woman's body. When we started trying to get pregnant, I was thirty-eight years old, physically fit, and active. I rejected my obstetrician's well-intentioned attempts to put me on fertility drugs; I couldn't understand his urgency. After all, we'd only just started trying. Weren't drugs a last resort for women who can't conceive? If I'd acted like the scientist I was and had consulted the scientific literature, however, I'd have popped the pills like candy.

Studies show that a woman's fertility drops rather rapidly after age thirty-one. On average, my chances of having a baby at age thirty-eight were less than half of what they were when I was twenty-five. Like many women, I'd fallen prey to the notion that I could put off having a family

Just because you follow your loves, it doesn't mean you are going to the land of "happily ever after."

until I was ready. I assumed I was still a good candidate for motherhood as long as I hadn't started menopause. But physiology has other plans and like all women over thirty-five, my eggs weren't as viable as those of a younger woman.

Two years later, I still hadn't conceived. Meanwhile, I was hoping to get a more permanent job at Auburn. The trouble was, my husband already had a job there. At first blush, his employment wouldn't seem to be an obstacle but in academia, "dual-career couples" like us often have difficulty getting jobs at the same institution. We both studied birds and even though I'd done a post-doc in genetics in an attempt to diversify my experience, we had done our graduate research on similar topics. Our Auburn colleagues urged us to seek a job offer from elsewhere to use as a bargaining chip. If another university wanted one of us, the reasoning went, Auburn would want to keep Douglas and, therefore, would offer me a job. Granted, this scenario was not quite the same as being wanted and valued for my own contributions, but at the time, I thought the strategy sounded like a fine plan.

When I spotted an open position at Oregon State University, I felt doubly hopeful. The job announcement included a phrase I'd never seen before: The university claimed to be "responsive to the needs of dual-career couples." Suddenly, the idea of moving to the Pacific Northwest took hold of me. From trips to Seattle, I already knew I loved the region. If Oregon State was progressive enough to offer jobs to both of us, maybe leaving Auburn would be worth the move. On the other hand, if an offer at another school motivated Auburn to make an offer to me, that would be great, too.

My optimism increased all the more when we attended an ornithology conference in Seattle. Two interesting events occurred during that trip. One was a chance conversation between Douglas and one of his colleagues who, as it turned out, was now at Oregon State. He invited Douglas to apply for the same job opportunity I'd identified a few weeks earlier. The other event was equally intriguing but harder to interpret.

I'd gone to Capitol Hill, a quirky Seattle neighborhood dotted with restaurants, coffee houses, and whimsical stores. Attracted by a giant Tibetan prayer wheel outside a shop called The Vajra, I walked into the small, spiritually-inspired gift shop. Why I thought that a tarot reading would shed light on my future, I can't say, but on a whim, I asked for one. The reader invited me back to a tiny room, rich with the odor of incense and decorated with Oriental tapestries. She laid out the cards in front of me and immediately pointed out two cards that fell in succession. "After the tower, comes the star," she said.

I snapped to attention and peered at the cards with intense interest. I'd only recently learned that my name, in both Hindi and Tibetan, means 'star.' The moment felt ripe with significance, even though I had no idea what the meaning might be. Afterward, I sat in a coffee shop on that late August afternoon of 2001 and scribbled down every detail of the reading that I could recall.

A few weeks later, back in Alabama, I was working in the lab on the morning of September 11, when one of my students came in to tell me that a plane had collided with the World Trade Center in New York City. On September the 12th, I sat in the Auburn University library and re-read my journal entry detailing my visit to The Vajra in Seattle. The words of the tarot reader echoed in my mind, "After the tower, the star."

Shortly afterward, Douglas was invited to interview at Oregon State. He got the job, and I was offered a position, too. Not a permanent professorial job, which was what I wanted, but a research position. When Auburn didn't make a counter-offer, we went house-hunting in Corvallis, Oregon.

LOOK FOR THE DOOR TO A FULLER LIFE

My tarot reading at The Vajra, where I heard the phrase "After the tower, the star," never would have happened had I not followed my intuition. It was my intuition, my gut, that insisted on pointing us toward the Pacific Northwest in our job search. If I'd failed to follow my inner wisdom, the opportunity to move west might never have materialized. Again, it was the quirky, the unexpected, and the slightly odd that provided an opening and led to a door that might have been missed—and would have remained closed—otherwise.

- Your obstacles and struggles have a lot to teach you about following your loves. What lessons have you been resisting? What insights have you embraced that can provide strength and encouragement?

- Traumatic events have a way of stripping us down, revealing the true essentials and necessities. While the events of September 11th didn't touch my life directly, like many Americans, that day marked a turning point. How did 9/11 affect your life—did any loves emerge for you after the Twin Towers fell? What other crises or traumatic events have stripped away your outer shell and opened you for growth?

- Look for quirky coincidences or unusual suggestions from your intuition. Start keeping a record of these and look for patterns or themes.

chapter three
The Unraveling at Midlife

People may call what happens at midlife "a crisis," but it's not. It's an unraveling—a time when you feel a desperate pull to live the life you want to live, not the one you're "supposed" to live. The unraveling is a time when you are challenged by the universe to let go of who you think you are supposed to be and to embrace who you are.

— BRENÉ BROWN

MIDLIFE OFTEN BRINGS abrupt shifts in perspective that challenge us to release old ways of being in favor of more authentic expressions of our Sexy + Soul-full selves. As unexpected circumstances forced me to let go of who I thought I was supposed to be, I discovered a new path to embrace who I really am.

LETTING GO OF WHO YOU THINK YOU'RE SUPPOSED TO BE

Within a few days of arriving in Corvallis, I was strolling around town, wearing a patchwork skirt I'd found at a boutique in "Portlandia," otherwise known as Portland, Oregon. My almost waist-length long hair was braided, coursing down my back. I was wearing my favorite pair of purple Birkenstock sandals. Unlike the days when I wore these kinds of clothes in Alabama, nobody stared at me. I no longer stood out. For the first time in my life, my inner loves were at home in my outer environment. Being in nature, caring about environmental issues, wearing unconventional clothing, taking my own bags to the grocery store—all business as usual here in the Pacific Northwest. I felt sexy—confident and bold—and I was certainly more soul-full, for soon after I arrived, I embraced my spiritual home in the Catholic church.

My spiritual life found full expression when I went to Mass at St. Mary Catholic Church for the first time. As I listened to the priest speak the words of consecration over the Eucharist, my heart was moved with so much love that I began to weep. I went through the Rite of Catholic Initiation for Adults and was confirmed at Easter in 2002.

By the time we'd been in Oregon for two years, however, it was becoming clear that my academic department wasn't as good a home for me as the town of Corvallis had turned out to be. For a while, I believed that my life might become the manifestation of my "star," that all the ambitions I'd nurtured since walking out of the rainforest and into graduate school would come to fruition after I reached my "tower." After all, the administrators of my ivory tower had promised me the opportunity of a permanent professorial job. All I had to do was work hard, be a good team player, and wait my turn.

Unfortunately, my plans started to unravel when I was 43. After suffering through the loss of my one pregnancy to miscarriage at age 41, my husband and I let go of the idea that we were meant to be parents.

But career-wise, I was not willing to let go of the dream of being a professor. Unfortunately, there were no upcoming job openings in my department. If we wanted to stay in Corvallis (which we did), and I wanted to hold the rank of professor (which I did), something had to give. Taking matters into my own hands, I went to my department head and boldly asked for what I wanted. Would he be willing to create a position for me so I could have a permanent job with the university? To my joy and relief, he said yes. However, yes wasn't what he meant.

A few weeks later, the faculty retreat was held. The topic of spousal hires was on the agenda for discussion. However, as soon as we arrived, I sensed that something was terribly wrong. The first hint was the department strategic plan in which another faculty spouse, a man who was also looking for a permanent job, was mentioned by name—while I was not. I found a seat in the back row while a feeling of dread settled in the pit of my stomach.

When the discussion commenced, I assumed that our department head would explain to the faculty his decision to open a position for me. But that's not what happened. Instead, without mentioning anyone by name, he introduced the topic of hiring spouses, asked what people thought of the idea, and then stood off to the side with a smirk on his face. The man everyone thought of as the department bully got up to speak. Looking over the heads of all my colleagues, the designated "truth teller" gazed directly into my eyes and, without preamble, delivered his message: "No matter what you do, no matter how hard you work, no matter how many students you advise or classes you teach, we will not hire you." He sat down. Not another word was spoken. And with that, the next topic on the agenda was brought up. Case closed.

As my husband and I got up to leave the room, he leaned over and whispered in my ear, "Don't give them the satisfaction of seeing you cry." It's the best advice anyone ever gave me.

One of the toughest coaching questions I know is, "What are you pretending not to know?" If I'd been working with a coach during the time leading up to that fateful faculty retreat, perhaps she'd have helped me ferret out all the truths I was ignoring in hopes they'd give up and go away. Some of the truths I pretended not to know were that my academic leader had a terrible habit of telling people what he thought they wanted to hear regardless of what he could actually deliver. I pretended not to know that I didn't fit well in my department. And—as I explained in the Introduction—I was overloaded and completely overwhelmed by my workload and I pretended not to know that, either.

After my public humiliation at the hands of my fellow faculty, I hid my head in shame. More specifically, I abandoned most of what I had been doing, started working from home, and avoided all my colleagues and friends from the university. Past experience taught me that when one member of a dual-career couple was rejected by the academic tribe, there were only a few options left. One was to leave—go to another university and try again. We'd already done that once and, besides, Corvallis was clearly the home of my soul; I wasn't about to move. Another option was to raise a stink

One of the toughest coaching questions I know is, "What are you pretending not to know?"

and force the issue. I'd seen other couples bring action against their universities with success, if you call success winning a discrimination suit to get a job in a department where you're not wanted. The third alternative? I had no idea.

Years before, Amos Bien suggested to me that I looked like a biologist and my heart had answered a resounding "Yes!" I knew that my heart hadn't been wrong. By following that "yes," I had found and married my soul-mate and I was living in the place where I felt the most at home. But I still had no answer to the question, "What next?"

Soon, I found myself grappling with a much more difficult question while on an airplane, returning to Panama where I'd spent four years preparing for a career path that I didn't have any more. When the flight attendant handed me an immigration form, I filled in little boxes with my *nombre* (Tara) and my *fecha de nacimiento* (November 25). And then I came to the blank labelled *ocupación*. Occupation, or that age-old question, "What do you do?" which often translates to: Who are you?

Tears began to well up in my eyes. My heart started aching. Within moments, I was sobbing. Thank goodness I was all alone in the back of the plane. I cried all the way through landing, baggage claim, and immigration. Ultimately, I left the space for occupation blank. I didn't know what to write. If I wasn't going to be a professor, I had no idea who I was anymore.

The next morning, I sat down with my journal and gazed out at the rainforest. It was in a rainforest like this where my life's journey had taken such a dramatic turn, from nursing and my horrible first marriage to biology and the love of my life. As a way of seeking perspective, I turned to a blank page and began listing my loves: nature, writing, learning, teaching, solitude, spirituality.

I'd worked with a life coach a few years before so I tried to ask myself the kinds of questions she'd asked me. What was I good at? What did I love doing? What activities made me feel the most alive? It was then that it occurred to me that I might like being a coach—a professional who works with people to help them realize their potential.

Coaching combines much of what I loved about being an academic: learning, teaching, mentoring. I could be independent—I didn't need an employer or even an office—so I could be my own boss and work from wherever I wanted. And best of all, I saw that coaching might allow me to take all the difficulties, struggles, and suffering I'd experienced and use them for someone else's benefit.

My path seemed so crooked. The twists and turns didn't seem to make sense. But somehow, in some strange way, I felt that I was on the right road. And that is when my journey out of academia to becoming a coach began.

I had to let go of who I thought I was supposed to be so that I could move forward. Letting go is one of the most difficult of actions, and yet, letting go is one of the great tasks of adulthood, especially as we age. As we grow older, we will be challenged to let go of many of our most treasured aspects of ourselves: our appearance, our physical capacities, our youth, to name a few. Letting go of my identity as an academic was extremely painful. I had to release both who I thought I was and who other people thought I was. Learning to let go of what people thought of me was an unlooked-for gift in this midlife time of unraveling.

LET GO OF WHO YOU THINK YOU ARE SUPPOSED TO BE

- Unraveling can be painful and, at the same time, productive. If you're in midlife, look for the frayed edges. What aspects of your life are threatening to come apart?

- By pretending not to know what was really going on, I missed many of the signals that my academic career was about to unravel. What are you pretending not to know about yourself and your loves?

- I experienced a lot of humiliation and embarrassment after my academic career unraveled. Forging a new identity, even one that was deeply rooted in my loves, was challenged by feelings of shame, like those I experienced when excavating the depths of my childhood. These feelings of shame may obscure your view of your loves. Claiming and owning your loves, even privately, can be of great help while you're recovering from an experience of unraveling. Take some time to brainstorm small acts of owning that you can undertake right now.

- While letting go of who you think you're supposed to be can be incredibly joyful and liberating, people around you may not be ready to let go of your old identity. When you're challenging the status quo, you're likely to run into some resistance. Whose boat will you be rocking? What obstacles will rise up between you and your loves when the unraveling occurs?

EMBRACING WHO YOU ARE

My loves, all of them, seem to have found a home. Situated as I am in the Pacific Northwest, my love of nature is easily satisfied and shared with my neighbors. My spirit has found a "resting place" in the Catholic church in which I worship, pray, grow, and serve. Artistically and creatively, my loves of beauty and art express themselves through mosaic, bookbinding, paper arts, and mixed-media painting. Love of learning, knowledge, and intellectual pursuits combine in service to my clients, where my love of teaching is joyously put to work. My soul-mate and I also celebrated twenty years of wedded bliss not long ago.

Letting go is one of the most difficult of actions, and yet, letting go is one of the great tasks of adulthood, especially as we age.

I've come a long way toward embracing who I am, yet I am still learning. Three years ago, my father died. Until then, I didn't have a clue of how many "daddy issues" I had. The season of grief after my dad's passing was complicated by a devastating blow dealt to me when my business partner decided to leave our coaching company. The day I entered therapy I explained my situation to my counselor ending with, "I have a lot of loss to deal with and if I don't face up to my stuff, it'll end up biting me in the ass."

One of my biggest issues was my inability to express my feelings directly. I didn't have control of my emotions; more often than not, they had control of me. A big turning point in my growth as a human being came when I realized that I could own my emotions and state aloud what I was feeling. I am still learning how to exercise direct, clear communication along with a robust vulnerability. I've come to see that being robustly vulnerable—tender hearted and tough skinned—allows me to be the most authentic in my relationships and my professional life. And I have the easiest time embracing who I am when I am being the real me.

Some days, I look at myself and see my post-menopause midriff paunch, the bags under my eyes, and the age spots on the backs of my hands. But more often than not, the woman I see looking at me isn't the fifty-something chick in the mirror. The woman I see in myself is whole and flawed,

Yearnings are often paradoxical & out of sync with your current life. If you're feeling drawn to oddities, those are likely to be signals of your soul's calling.

broken and beautiful, sexy and soul-full. In some miraculous way, I've come to feel genuine affection for myself—I have a real appreciation for my strengths and my weaknesses, my experience and my expertise. In spite of all the ups and downs I've been through, I love who I am and I wouldn't change a thing about what it took to get me here.

At each turn in my journey, my loves accompanied me. At times, they were hidden. On occasion, I allowed them to be stolen. But each and every time, they returned themselves to me with the same loyal persistence of a homing dove who flies through storms yet somehow, someway, gets back home. Discovering (and re-discovering) my loves was pivotal in the process of embracing who I am.

{Welcoming Your Loves}

How CAN you, too, welcome the arrival of these tireless travelers: your loves?

Step 1: Cultivate an Awareness of Your Soul-full Yearnings

Artist and self-proclaimed "possibilitarian," Kelly Rae Roberts tells of how the "loudest, most pesky whisper" in her journey to being a professional artist had nothing to do with art. Instead, she felt called to start running. That's exactly the kind of oddball message I heard at various times in my life, which you might hear, too. It seems that our bodies often speak to us—pay attention to what your physical self seems to most want and need. Don't ignore these "whispers" just because they don't make sense. Your loves sometimes must use the strangest of means to get your attention.

Cultivate an awareness of the yearnings of your soul. These longings differ from wants and needs. Yearnings are often paradoxical and out of sync with your current life. If you're feeling drawn to oddities, especially if those are far outside your current norms, like bird watching was for me or running was for Kelly Rae Roberts, those are likely to be signals of your soul's calling.

Step 2: Follow Where Your Yearnings Lead You

Gently follow the calling of your yearnings. This step sometimes requires great courage. In embracing your loves (the deepest of which is true self-love), you may not go through changes as profound and life-altering as some of the ones I've experienced. But even your more ordinary loves can, at times, be very threatening to your status quo.

Cultivate faith and trust. Seek supportive, yet objective, companions: A coach, spiritual director, counselor, or other helping professional can give you guidance and provide a safe environment for your hopes and dreams, during these often confusing and challenging times.

Step 3: Keep Going

I once had an engraved bracelet that bore the message, "Stay loyal to your journey." At any point in my life, I could have called it quits. Literally. I pray with all my heart that you will never know despair as deep as I have felt at times in my life, but given how many women suffer from depression, you have probably had some terrible experiences. You may even have been tempted to end your life. Even if you've never been suicidal, there is a huge temptation to simply give up and quit trying. Creating a life around your loves takes courage and time.

Even the most accomplished and admired women struggle ·
feeling that things will never quite work out for them. The b
I've heard on this topic is: "...If you are ever in any way disc
entreat you to cast this away...never allow your spirit to ar

in any way to any anxiety or downheartedness to which you feel inclined," writes St. Francis de Sales (who himself knew much failure and desolation). "Never under any pretext whatsoever [should you] yield to the temptation of discouragement..."

In your journey, you may also encounter fear. What I've learned is that when the fear comes, even though I feel a very real sense of dread right down in the pit of my stomach, I must firmly lead myself straight toward it. I know this kind of fear is not protecting me; instead, the fear is preventing me from being united with my loves.

Facing fear has taught me to be gentle with myself. Gentle as in: learning to unclench, relax, and allow. This is quite different from forcing, pushing, and making myself do things I'm afraid to do or not ready to try yet. We're called to strike a balance between being gentle with ourselves and still remaining loyal to the journey. The only way to find that balance is to keep going.

Even the most accomplished and admired women struggle with the feeling that things will never quite work out for them.

Rather than tell you to "Try, try again," however, I counsel you to listen for your soul's calling. Look for the small invitation. Be aware of the incongruous pull of the oddity. Those almost always signal that something you love is nearby.

SURRENDERING TO WHAT IS

What if your love still eludes you even after you've excavated the depths exploring your childhood, unearthed the shards of your (teen) spirit, reassembled the fragments of your whole self, and yearned your way toward doors? What if you have you let go of who you think you're supposed to be and embraced who you are and you still haven't (re)discovered your loves?

If all else fails in your search to reveal to yourself what you love, give yourself permission to be fallow. Let the inner, invisible work take place; it sets the stage for more visible outer work later. Take walks. Read books—novels, poetry, spiritual wisdom. Dig in your garden. Clean your house. These actions may look as if you're not seeking your love but that's not the case.

Growth occurs after seasons of fallow. You can trust that ancient rhythm. It will not fail you.

Author Byron Katie says that the way we know that things are supposed to be a certain way is because that is how they are. If circumstances were supposed to be different, they would be. Grasping the truth of Byron Katie's advice is a relief. This is how it's supposed to be now—that you don't yet know what you love. Find comfort knowing that if that's the way it is, that's how it's supposed to be—for now.

Consider bringing yourself to a point of surrender. Not surrender as in "lost the battle" or being overpowered by some force stronger than yourself. No. This is a completely safe form of surrender that allows you to accept yourself and your situation as it is now. Your acceptance doesn't mean that you give up on change or the idea that one day things will be different. Acceptance means "loving what is," as Byron Katie so wisely encourages us to do. This form of surrender relaxes the clenched muscles and allows any tightness gripping your heart to unfurl and decompress. From that point of ease, which may take a little while to occur, answers will reveal themselves.

In 2010, Elizabeth Gilbert celebrated her second *New York Times* bestseller when her memoir, *Committed*, hit the shelves. Gilbert's first book, *Eat, Pray, Love* was phenomenally successful, from its selection by Oprah's Book Club all the way to the big screen, where Gilbert herself was played by megawatt star Julia Roberts. But the success of *Committed* almost didn't happen.

After years of researching and drafting the entire manuscript, Gilbert realized that it was terrible. Unpublishable. In her own words, "crap." Not only was her book a mess, Gilbert herself was completely fried. With no desire to continue slaving away, she quit struggling with writing and surrendered, spending her summer on something completely different: gardening. Some months after giving up on her manuscript, while absentmindedly tending the tomatoes, she suddenly knew exactly how to fix the book. After scraping the dirt out from under her fingernails, she scurried back to the keyboard and revised her manuscript into the bestseller it became.

I know this kind of allowing is so different from what productivity experts usually counsel; it is the opposite of action. But that's part of the unique gift of Sexy + Soul-full Productivity. Your journey can be as much about acknowledging and embracing inaction and ease as it is about throwing yourself into joyful effort and action.

The opposite of ease is struggle. Struggle is action but ineffective action—a futile exertion that gets you nowhere. Early in 2013, I pitched an earlier version of this book to a publisher. The proposal was rejected, not because the publisher didn't like the book, but because I wasn't "famous" enough. Afterward, I entered a period of struggle about what to do next. This struggle felt like a wrestling match wherein I went back and forth without making any progress in either direction. My teeth were clenched, my back was tight, and my hands were curled into fists. I was fighting an incredibly intense internal battle. Should I write the book anyway? Should I give up? I expended a lot of effort but not much actually happened. That's the definition of struggle.

The struggle ended when I decided to surrender. I let go of worry, let go of striving, let go of trying to figure the solutions out. And after surrendering, all sorts of solutions and opportunities started to come to me. I asked myself: What does hope and possibility look like? I followed my intuition about what actions optimism might counsel in my circumstance. After only a few weeks, the inspiration for *Sexy + Soul-full* came to me. The whole approach was out of the ordinary for productivity books; the approach was feminine and quirky and outside the box. In other words, just right for me!

Being still, listening for your own soul's voice, is never a waste of time. Practice courage in surrender. Your loves are seeking you just as strongly as you are seeking them. Sometimes it is you that must be found, rather than the other way round.

In her prayer for the fallow times, Heather King writes, "Help me to accept myself the way I am [without] giving up the idea of healing and growth..." Not giving up that there might be something that you can do, some action that you can take, some love you can embrace, but giving up on the idea that you have to know everything and know it now.

*Being still, listening for your
own soul's voice, is never a waste
of time.*

Part II

Make Time for What You Love

For me, and for many of us, our first waking thought of the day is "I didn't get enough sleep." The next one is "I don't have enough time."

— Lynne Twist

It was a bright, sunny spring day in Tacoma, Washington, when I made my way up to my hotel room and gazed out the window overlooking the Puget Sound. In the distance, I could see dozens of sailboats skimming over the glittering waves. I sat down at the desk and dialed in to the conference line to greet the callers for my podcast, the GTD Virtual Study Group.

I'd founded the podcast some six years earlier as a way of enhancing my own productivity education. To my astonishment, our listenership skyrocketed and people called in from around the world to join the twice-monthly conversations. On that particular day, I was hosting a round-table of experts along with our usual group of *Getting Things Done* enthusiasts. As the invited participants called in, I greeted them and exchanged pleasantries.

One of the productivity gurus, a fellow I'll call Paul, was calling in from the Seattle region, and I mentioned that I was in town.

"I'm attending the Society of American Mosaic Artists conference— I'm a mosaicist," I said.

A long pause followed. The silence was so prolonged that I began to wonder if he'd gotten cut off. Finally, he replied, "Oh!"

Now it was my turn to hesitate. Oh? What did he mean by Oh? Another caller interrupted the pause, and only after the call did I come up with an interpretation for Paul's lukewarm response. I think he was surprised that making art was a priority for me. After all, the norm in the productivity world was (and still is) to put career and work life ahead of everything.

Making time for what you love, unapologetically and joyfully, is one of the principles that sets Sexy + Soul-full apart from productivity as usual. I believe that once you've (re)discovered what you love, you should have the freedom to pursue that love with zeal! However, after encountering your loves, you may find yourself feeling stuck—mired in choices and circumstances that no longer suit how you would like to invest in yourself. You need breathing room so you can make time for what (and who) you love.

As I have apprenticed myself to the alchemy of time, my whole life has completely shifted and changed. I went from putting work ahead of everything—ahead of my marriage, my relationships, and even my own health—to enjoying putting my loves first and placing my work in service of those loves. By making time for what I love, I've learned that I have the power to shape my days and reap fulfillment and satisfaction from my efforts. I can't wait to share these lessons with you so that you, too, can begin to make time for what you love.

But what if you haven't yet (re)discovered your loves? By undertaking the three apprenticeships in the alchemy of time, you will give yourself room to stretch your wings and open your soul. Often, life is so densely packed that there are too many obstacles in the way to allow you to see what's possible. By making time for what you love, you'll

> *Making time for what you love, unapologetically and joyfully, is one of the principles that sets Sexy + Soul-full apart from productivity as usual.*

be affirming your faith and nurturing the belief that your loves are awaiting you, even if you can't quite make out their outlines yet. So don't despair! Keep taking one small step after another and trust that you'll arrive at the knowledge of your loves when the moment is right for them to emerge.

In this part of the book, I'll acquaint you with three destructive myths about time and then, I'll provide you with a path to rejecting each one. You won't just discard these myths, however. You'll replace them with three helpful and effective truths about time. To make the switch, you'll undertake simple tasks in three apprenticeships in the alchemy of time.

In your apprenticeship to *enough,* you'll learn that you have enough time now. I'll supply you with skills to practice that will give you valuable experience in experiencing enough and escaping the clutches of scarcity.

Whether you realize it or not, time is what you think (and say) it is. You'll gain the ability to mold your perception of time and exert greater control over your experiences of time during your apprenticeship to ease. The practices of mindfulness, changing how you talk about time, and honoring stillness will surprise you with gifts of freedom and independence from the clock.

The destructive myth "My time is precious," will undergo a subtle but extremely powerful makeover in the last chapter of this part of the book. The lessons of generosity, letting go, and welcoming will change what it means to possess time.

In the opening quote, Lynne Twist articulates that waking thought that most people have: "I don't have enough time." Imagine what it would be like to wake up with a completely different point of view.

What if you woke up every morning knowing that you got enough rest and that you have enough time to do what you want to do? And not only that, but you have the ease and the equanimity to enjoy every day, no matter what your schedule is like? By rejecting the three destructive myths about time, you can inhabit this new perspective as your very own, and sooner than you think! Let's get started.

chapter four
Three Destructive Myths About Time

"I DON'T HAVE TIME!" wailed my client, Alicia. "My schedule is wall to wall. I'm completely slammed. And I just got an email inviting me to a reception honoring one of my colleagues. I simply *must* go. But honestly, I can't. I shouldn't. But I must."

"So if you don't have time, why not decline the invitation? You could send a card or a nice bouquet," I replied.

"Oh, I can't decline. I *have* to be there."

"And so how will you make that happen?" I asked.

"Well, I'll make the time!" she said.

This short conversation was typical of a coaching session with Alicia, an incredibly talented, hard-working mom and prestigious thought-leader. Her language (and probably her thoughts, too) were expressions of how her time felt and behaved. The clock was Alicia's enemy, with time passing far too quickly. Her calendar was crammed far too full. And she was "out of time." And yet, she was constantly "making time" for everyone and everything except her loves: her family, her spiritual life, and her self-care. If she made time for her own loves, which was rarely, she felt guilty and embarrassed, as if she was doing something terribly wrong.

Alicia had hired me to help her learn to manage her time and tasks better. But the biggest problem, besides her unwillingness to say "no," was her unstated belief in the three myths about time. Through my work with this client and hundreds of other people seeking greater control over their time, and thus, their lives, I've discovered a widespread acceptance of three destructive myths about time.

These three myths drive all sorts of behaviors and decisions which, inevitably, don't help matters because the intended solutions are aimed at addressing the problem from the wrong direction. It's not that all the time and task management experts are wrong or that the abundant productivity advice, hacks, tips, and tricks don't work. It's that by leaving these myths unchallenged, and assuming that they represent the truth, we remain stuck in a distorted relationship with time.

Myth #1: I will have more time later.

The first of the three myths about time is "I will have more time later."

This is one of the most common beliefs about time, regardless of how savvy or productive you might be. When you look at your schedule today or glance ahead to the next couple of weeks, you're likely to see that you're booked solid. You have some idea (even if it might be a bit vague) about what's coming up and how much of your time will be required to do it. But if you gaze farther ahead into the future, say six months or year from now, your schedule (most likely) looks blissfully open. This unscheduled space on the calendar leaves you with the notion that not now, *but later*, in the future, you'll have more time—more time to devote to your loves, your family, and yourself. Many people actually don't use any rational evidence to support their idea that they'll have more time later, and in fact, may not even be conscious of this belief and how it controls their behavior. But the myth is hard at work in the background, nonetheless.

One symptom that you're living under the influence of this myth is when you experience the "yes-damn" phenomenon. You probably know the "yes-damn" scenario quite well: You get an invitation to give a presentation at work in the (relatively) far future. At the time you receive the invite, you're crazy busy but you can easily see yourself being well-prepared and fulfilling your commitment on this safely far-in-the-future date. So you happily crow, "Yes!" But when the time for the presentation draws near, you experience the "damn" moment as you realize you're *still* totally slammed. *Dammit! What was I thinking when I said "yes?"* you moan, as you are hit with the full weight of the "yes-damn" phenomenon. Most likely you were thinking (even if not consciously) that the myth was true, that you'd actually have more time later. But a myth is a myth for a reason; it's not true: You will *not* have more time later.

The myth also works against you in other ways. Imagine you've just moved to a wonderful new city, one you've longed to visit and enjoy, let's say Paris. If you were on your way to Paris for a two-week vacation, you'd make the most of your all-too-short time there. You'd plan every moment so as to see many works of art, eat many delectable meals, sip lots of glasses of wine, and gaze at the view from the Eiffel Tower (and don't forget to take a selfie at the Arc de Triomphe!).

But if you were going to be in Paris permanently, you'd be overwhelmed with the move and the myth would whisper that you'd have more time later. And lo, months after your arrival, you'd find that visitors from home are coming and you're going with them to the Louvre for the first time, even though you've been in Paris for how long? I've been just as guilty of giving in to this myth as anyone else: You'd wouldn't believe how much of my home state of Oregon I have yet to see, all because I, too, have assumed that I will have plenty of time later to do so.

Psychologists who study the effects of the myth of more time later, which they've dubbed "resource slack," point out that people put off all kinds of things, like spending gift certificates and visiting local landmarks, all because of the faulty assumption that while they're too busy right now, they'll have time for such things...later.

How many moments of our lives slip past because of this myth? Think about all the times you've put off going to see a friend or a family member. All the invitations you've turned down. All the opportunities you've lost. What dreams are you putting off because you assume that you'll have time for them later?

The myth of more time later is not just a psychological issue but a spiritual one as well. "When we believe we are not where we need to be for spiritual growth, we relegate our daily life to a secondary tier. We energetically pull out of our spiritual life and wait for the appropriate secluded moment in order to fully engage," writes meditation teacher, Rodney Smith. Of course, the "appropriate secluded moment" is almost always in the future, at some later time. And this is precisely where the myth of having more time later does its greatest damage.

Smith continues, "Leaning toward or away from any experience creates an anticipation of fulfillment in the future, and the sacred that exists here and now is lost."

For years, I would look at some task or opportunity or momentary delight, and say to myself, "I don't have time for that right now." I operated under the myth of more time later, along with my false assumption that I needed large blocks of uninterrupted time in order to do what I love. Then one day, I asked myself, "When will you have time? It's always 'right now!'" This was the beginning of my awakening about this terribly powerful myth. "We cannot delay fully embracing the [now] moment," adds Smith. "To do so maintains the divisions within the mind, the division between the mind and the body, and the division between the organism and its environment. All divisions are attempts to keep us from the truth of what is right here. When this is understood...there can be no more hesitation, no more postponement, and no more pulling back and waiting for a more opportune time. It is literally now or never."

Centuries ago, St. Ignatius of Loyola advised, "We should never postpone a good work, no matter how small it may be, with the thought of later doing something greater. It is a very common temptation of the enemy to be always placing before us the perfection of things to come [later] and bring us to make little of the present." He, too, knew about this myth of more time later, and placed the blame on "the enemy," who was, in his view, Satan himself. Whether or not you agree with his choice of where to put the blame, the veracity of his observation remains. The myth whispers that sometime later your schedule will be more open and thus, you can put off doing your good work until then.

One of the dangers of this myth is that it can become a habitual temptation—that is, something that ceaselessly siphons off energy, motivation, and industriousness. One of the names for this kind of temptation is acedia—a very old word that comes from the experiences of holy men and women who lived deeply spiritual lives in the deserts, during the first few centuries after the time of Christ.

Typically, these spiritual seekers lived in small communities or as hermits where they prayed and studied scripture. Even though such a life might sound uncomplicated, these holy ones found that they were attacked by feelings that their work was unimportant or irrelevant. They experienced extreme restlessness and bouts of boredom, sleepiness, and apathy. They had trouble keeping their minds on the work at hand, whether it was caring for the needs of their fellow monks and the poor, or holding their thoughts up to God. They ascribed these difficulties to the "noonday devil" who tempted and teased and discouraged the unwary, drawing them away from their heavenly pursuits. And acedia's favorite ploy was to whisper: "Later. Not now, you're too tired. Not now, you aren't spiritual enough. Not now....later."

Even though the concept of acedia has fallen into disuse, the experience of it is still very much alive and well. The Greek root of the word acedia means "absence of care," or put another way: not caring, not giving a damn. It's a sense of nihilism—that all is useless and pointless. Acedia is not depression, which is a much more emotional and, often, a biochemical disorder. No, acedia is a sort of progressive apathy that whispers to you that nothing you do will be of much significance, so why bother? In my experience, acedia is often a side effect of the "more time later" myth, which counsels constant delay and procrastination rather than acting now.

The key to freeing yourself from this myth is to first realize that it's a lie. However, the vast landscape of having more time to do what you love isn't a mirage. There is enough time, not in the future, but right now. Before you can enjoy the experience of enough time now however, you must bust the other two myths about time.

MYTH #2: TIME IS OUTSIDE MY CONTROL.

The second myth about time is "Time is outside my control."

This myth finds its deep roots buried in how we measure time using clocks and calendars. It is true that time is a great equalizer: Everyone gets the same number of hours each day; we all use the same calendar with days and dates and years marked out for all to abide by. From this perspective, the myth of time being outside our control would seem to be true. However that's not at all the case.

As bizarre and hard to grasp as it may seem, according to cutting edge physics, time may not actually exist at all. Some physicists say that the concept of time as a progressive, sequential passage along a three bus-stop line—past, now, and future—isn't true. It's all just "now." Yep, everything that has happened or will happen is occurring right now. This makes the now-moment even more amazing because it's where *everything* is happening. Literally everything from the big bang to the dinosaurs to the premier of Season 1,000 of Game of Thrones. So if that's the case, and time as we know it doesn't exist, it's even more freaky that we experience time as sequential with a past, present, and future.

Neurophysiologists say our brains manufacture our experiences of time. Mostly, this process of creation is outside our conscious control. But not always. "Time is this rubbery thing," says neuroscientist David Eagleman. "It stretches out when you really turn your brain resources on." Put another way, when you're fully present and engaged with the world around you, your brain assumes that time is passing more slowly and that you have more of it.

But here's the real kicker, "[The] less information your brain writes down, the more quickly time seems to pass," says Eagleman. As you go faster and faster, rushing around like the proverbial headless chicken, your brain can no longer pick up the finer details of the world around you. That means your brain is taking in less information, and you will perceive time as passing more quickly. Quite simply, your brain—by using the amount of detailed information it receives—is creating your perception of time.

Not only does your brain's wiring play a central role in your experience of time, your time truly is what you think it is and it behaves how you say it does. However it is that you imagine your time to be—scarce or abundant, speeding or dragging, standing still or running out—you create your own experience through how you think about your time and what you say aloud about it.

Take, for example, the client I introduced you to at the beginning of the chapter. All of Alicia's language pointed to a deeply felt experience of time as short, scarce, limited, lacking, and inadequate. Her time was passing too quickly, there was never enough of it, and she was constantly running out of what little time she had. She used the same phrases over and over, mantras like: "I don't have time;" "I'm short on time;" and

"I don't have enough time." These expressions of angst were almost certainly representative of what she was thinking, too. Her repeated exclamations not only did nothing to help her cope with the tremendous demands under which she labored, but, in fact, contributed to the way she experienced her time in the first place. Her words about time were true, in that they helped create her reality vis à vis her perception of time. For perception, largely, *is* reality.

The consequence of believing that time is outside our control is that we abdicate our power to manage our *experience* of time. By dismissing how much control we actually have, we not only lose the ability to create a more enjoyable and powerful experience of our time, but we actually create experiences for ourselves that are self-defeating and make time behave in ways we'd rather it didn't. This is part of the reason many time management strategies fail: None of the interventions address this curious yet real phenomenon of our ability to stretch, shrink, speed up, or slow down this malleable thing called time.

But before you begin to mold your time, there is one more myth to address.

Myth #3: My time is precious.

The third myth about time is "My time is precious."

This is the most shocking and counter-intuitive myth of them all because it is bandied about constantly and sounds so wise and profound and truthy. There are a number of variations on this myth that run along the same lines: "Life is short," "My time is valuable," "I hate wasting my time." All of these statements harken back to the original mythic notion of our time as an exceedingly precious, valuable resource. However, deep down, most of us know this myth is a bunch of hooey. One only has to look at how we actually use our time to see that we don't believe that our time is precious at all. How many hours have we wasted in the past seven days engaged in meaningless, pointless activities or purely frittering away our time on Facebook, Twitter, or some silly game? (And yes, I can be just as guilty of this as anyone else, much to my chagrin.) But the truth is, this idea that our time is precious is merely a fabrication, a sweet lie that we tell ourselves.

This myth does, however, contain an important kernel of truth. Time, as a currency, *is* precious, worth far more than money. Money can be saved, banked, stashed away for later. Not time! Time is constantly on the move; no matter how you spend or perceive it, you only have twenty-four hours a day. And not only are the hours finite, but your time on earth is, too. None of us knows how many days will be allotted to our lives but we all know that our lives will end. And not only our lives, but our families' and friends' and pets' lives, too. All of us are mortal and ephemeral.

Yet, paradoxically, time is also abundant. Unlike money, where you often run low, your time is constantly being replenished. Every day you get another twenty-four hours—one thousand, four hundred, and forty minutes—to use as you'd like. Your time is abundant enough to share, to give freely, and to spend on what (and with who) you love; that is, if you're solidly grounded in your understanding that this myth isn't true.

But what's the problem? Accepting this myth would seem harmless. After all, if you know your time is precious, wouldn't that be a good thing? Unfortunately, there are as many problems with taking this myth to heart as there are with pretending as if it's true while paying the usual meaningless lip service to it.

The difficulty with taking this myth to heart is that it leads people to overvalue their time. You must be shaking your head at me by now. After all, if you knew your time was incredibly precious, you'd not waste a minute! You'd be ever so much more careful and industrious and surely, you'd be very productive and fabulous. And that may be true, but all that fabulousness would likely come with a hefty price tag.

Psychologists who study human behavior have noticed a disturbing problem with the folks who value their own time too highly: They are often extremely impatient. One clever study took a close look at how feelings of entitlement affected both behavior and perception of time. For their experiment, the researchers asked students to complete a deliberately dull survey. They primed the students with two sets of instructions. Some students were told that the survey was a simple assessment of preferences. The other group was told that the survey was being conducted because "You're entitled to the best possible experiences here on campus." Afterward, both groups were asked how much time it took to complete the survey. The entitlement-primed group thought that the survey took two and a half minutes longer than did students who weren't primed as entitled—which, undoubtedly, felt like an eternity (and which, again, goes to show how malleable the experience of time is). In actuality, both groups completed the survey in the same amount of time.

The researchers repeated the study and gave a new set of students similar tests. In this go-round, the entitlement messages were delivered subliminally—the entitlement-primed students couldn't consciously make out the words on their computer screens (words such as: special, better, deserve, me, mine, etc.) but they reacted in just the same way as the overtly entitlement-primed students had. For those primed to feel entitled, time crawled when presented with a dull task. And get this: The entitlement-primed participants were in a much bigger hurry to leave the laboratory—they walked significantly faster than the control group when departing. It was as if they just couldn't stand to waste another second of their all-too-precious time.

The effects of valuing one's time by equating it to money has even greater negative effects on people's attitudes and behavior. Researchers asked participants to put a dollar value on their time. The higher the dollar amount assigned to their hours, the less likely participants were to donate their time to others, such as in volunteer activities. In other words, valuing their time as precious in the monetary sense made participants feel more selfish and act more stingy.

Ultimately, the myth of time as precious is based in a comparison mindset. Comparison looks for less than versus more than. In the case of time, we tend to make these comparisons along the lines of "My time is precious" with the unspoken, "and yours is not." These kinds of comparisons can lead us to not just overvalue our own time or to devalue other people's time, but to devalue the people themselves.

One colleague of mine, in talking about his baby daughter told me, "I love her and everything but...she takes up too much of my time." That "but" was the balance on which her worth was compared and found wanting: His too-precious time was more valuable than caring for his own child.

Before you dismiss this example as too extreme, think about how many workplace cultures punish those who dare to put time with their families over their careers. In academia, there's even a derogative name for it: the Mommy Track. Unlike the tenure track, which is occupied by serious scholars who take their serious academic careers seriously, the Mommy Track is for women who dare to have families. I've heard dozens of female graduate students and professors recount horror stories of workplace prejudice, all of which is predicated on the notion that when a woman makes family a priority (particularly by daring to have one in the first place), she can't possibly be a good professor or researcher. In fact, considering time spent on work as more precious than time spent on family, rest, or play, is so commonplace that it hardly goes without saying. Sadly, I, too, used to believe that time spent working was more valuable than everything and everyone else.

So if your time isn't precious, what is? We will take on the subtle distinctions that will allow you to escape the clutches of this myth in your apprenticeship to equanimity. As you prepare to debunk this and the other two myths about time, you might want to become acquainted with the big lie from which all three myths spring. This is the lie of scarcity.

THE BIGGEST LIE: SCARCITY

Scarcity, or the dogma of never enough, is the lie that gives rise to these three destructive myths about time.

If we are in state of "more later" (implying that there is not enough now), powerlessness (that is, lack of control), and comparison (weighing alternatives and finding that something is less than, or not enough), we are under the influence of the lie of scarcity. In fact, the scarcity lie is what all time management strategies, and for that matter, the entire field of personal productivity, are predicated upon. Time is limited—the presupposition runs—you do not have enough of it (and you never will), there is not enough of you to go around (and never will be), and thus, you must strain to get more out of your share of this finite resource.

Scarcity naturally begets fear. If there is not enough, then you are constantly in danger of running out or going wanting. Unlike the kind of danger that is real and concrete (like a saber-toothed tiger or a gun-toting robber), this kind of danger is invisible and without substance. It's the kind of thing that wakes you up at night and then, in the morning, you can't remember exactly what you were worried about. But worry, you do. And worry is extraordinarily powerful in its ability to distract you from what matters and what's real. This stress is not just a psychological problem but a spiritual one as well.

Scarcity draws us out of the sacred present-moment and focuses attention on an imagined and potentially disastrous future. Instead of encouraging trust and faith, scarcity counsels doubt and distrust. Distrust naturally leads to disconnection, which sets the stage for alienation, isolation, and conflict. Scarcity leads us into competition with each other and ignites our "hustle for worthiness."

Here's how to dance the hustle for worthiness: Scarcity tells you that you are not enough now, and you must be more to have some chance of being enough in the future (a variation on the first myth about time). *Being more* usually gets translated into *doing more*. Because you are not enough, you can never do enough to become enough. This leads to an ongoing tap dance of overcommitment, workaholism, and a super-sized ambition that is never satiated...because you are never enough. This dance of never enough has obvious implications for how we spend our time.

When we are in the talons of the delusion of scarcity, we prioritize accomplishment over practically everything else and especially over self-care, our loved ones, rest, and play. In terms of time, this chase almost always results in living life at a heightened velocity, which we know from neuroscience, only makes time speed by even more quickly. Life, on fast forward, creates more isolation and alienation. Poet David Whyte explains, "The trouble with velocity ... is after a while, you cannot perceive anything or anyone that isn't traveling at the same speed as you are...And things that move according to a slower wave form actually seem to become enemies to you and enemies to your way of life. You get quite disturbed by people who are easy with themselves and easy with life and [who] aren't charging around like you do."

Rejecting this lie of scarcity is one of the most powerful acts you can ever undertake, because you will not only be freed to experience your time differently but you will be liberated in practically every other area of your life as well. I won't be asking you to reject scarcity all at once, however, because the lie is so interwoven into the fabric of our lives that I'd be leaving you naked! Instead, I'm inviting you reject scarcity while you debunk the three destructive myths about time through learning the alchemy of time.

As you may already know, alchemy is an ancient art which proposed to take common items and turn them into valuable rarities. While converting lead into gold turned out to be impossible, the alchemy of time is wonderfully effective. You will learn the alchemy of time through three apprenticeships: to enough, to ease, and to equanimity. In your apprenticeships, you'll take these unhelpful and destructive myths about time and turn them into effective behaviors that will allow you to make time for what (and who) you love.

As is true in all apprenticeships, you'll be asked to carry out small, yet essential, activities that slowly build toward mastery. In olden times, apprentices started with sweeping the floors and other jobs that were easy to do and kept them (and the master's work) out of harm's way. Some of what you undertake in your apprenticeship in the alchemy of time may, at first, seem similarly simplistic. And yet, with practice, these uncomplicated ways of being will become your most valuable tools in living the productive life of a Sexy + Soul-full woman.

One by one, you will take on each myth about time.

- "I will have more time later" will be transformed into "I have enough time now."

- "Time is outside my control" will morph into "Time is what I think it is."

- "My time is precious" will undergo a subtle, yet extreme, makeover to "All time is precious."

chapter five

I Have Enough Time Now: An Apprenticeship to Enough

"I WILL HAVE more time later" is the first of the three myths about time that will undergo transformation on your journey to Sexy + Soul-full. As you work with the alchemy of time, you will discard this myth so as to experience enough time now. I realize that you may have difficulty believing that there will ever be enough time! Your disbelief (and perhaps downright skepticism) is, no doubt, backed up by plenty of evidence: Your over-full schedule, your bulging calendar, and your frazzled nerves all stand in mute testament to the scarcity of your time.

As you learned in the previous chapter, scarcity exerts a profound and pernicious influence. To counter scarcity's effects, during this phase of your development as a Sexy + Soul-full woman, you will be apprenticed to scarcity's opposite: enough.

WHAT DOES IT MEAN TO BE APPRENTICED TO ENOUGH?

First, let's talk about how I define apprentice. An apprentice is someone who has humbled herself to become a beginner, is willing to be child-like in her approach to learning, a blank slate upon which mastery can eventually be written.

Most of us are more familiar with another state of being that is quite different from that of an apprentice. My own take on a classic Buddhist teaching story puts it this way:

A very learned woman came to have tea with the master. As the master quietly went about preparing the brew, the learned woman examined the master's library and exclaimed over books she herself had written and authors of whom she approved. The learned woman spouted off her opinions of this idea and that philosophy, carefully framing her arguments in the most impressive possible way. When the master motioned silently for her to come to the table, the learned woman went on and on about the china and how it was manufactured, the tea and her visits to the regions where it was grown, and the effects of global climate change on the world economy.

As the rich, steamy aroma of the tea finally permeated her consciousness, she noticed that the master was pouring her tea. And the tea kept splashing into her cup until it was overflowing! Tea cascaded over the table and on to the floor, soaking her kimono with warmth, which quickly changed to chill as it dripped over her legs and puddled in her slippers. The learned woman was aghast (and for a blissful moment, silent) but finally recovered her presence of mind to shout, "Stop! Stop! Can't you see that the cup is full?"

The master stopped pouring the tea and carefully set the pot into the lake of tea on the table top. Leaning back, the master smiled and said, "Yes, when the cup is full, there is no room for more." The learned woman knew exactly what the master meant: she, herself, was full—not just with knowledge but with her own self-importance—so much that she had no room to learn anything from the master.

Like the learned woman in the story, we may also be very full. Full of knowledge and experience, full of regret and heartache, full of effort and ambition. There are so many ways to be full! And meanwhile, scarcity is telling us that we still don't have enough! In so many often paradoxical and contradictory ways, scarcity argues that we don't have enough time nor do we have enough in our lives. Scarcity says that we must run faster and work harder to get more. But where exactly would we put this more?

Just as the learned woman's tea cup was full and overflowing, flooding the table and soaking down to her Spanx, we, too, are flooded and running over with unpleasant, and at times disastrous, consequences. To become an apprentice, therefore, there must be a kind of emptying out so that there is space for something new. And that something new will be enough.

How Will You Experience Enough Right Now?

Enough is a rather amazing concept: Neither more than is needed nor less than is necessary. In that sense, enough is a very precise quantity. At the same time, the concept of enough is extremely expansive. From the perspective of enough, there is great possibility and freedom. Try this little visualization exercise with me to see what I mean.

The visualization exercise gives you a glimpse of what you'll be doing in your apprenticeship: You'll undertake small, simple acts that

Visualization

Take a moment to breathe deeply and to be fully present in your body. Imagine that you are sitting at a table in a lovely coffee shop. A soft gray light is coming through the window behind you. The murmur of conversation is layered with the sounds of The Eagles singing "Witchy Woman." The air is a comfortable temperature and perfumed with the scent of coffee and gingerbread. Your shoulders feel heavy and relaxed as your wrists rest on the keyboard and your fingers tap the keys of your laptop. You are conscious of your breath, and all that's around you. And suddenly you feel that sense of contentment that signals *enough right now*. There is enough space, time, and creativity to do your work. Not in some future moment, but right now, here. Drink in that feeling, and notice the calm sense of latent energy that underlies *enough right now*.

give you the experience of enough right now. At first, these moments of enough right now will be rather fleeting. It's like that moment of doing a handstand. You find yourself balanced for a split second and then you'll be back where you started. But with practice, it gets easier and easier to find that balance point and hold it, breathe, and enjoy the sensation of being upside down. Yoga inversions are actually a really good metaphor for enough right now because, like a handstand, you're turning the usual way of doing things upside down. Scarcity says, "There is no time now; I will have more time later." Enough right now flips the situation on its head and says, "There is enough time now; there is no later." (And this is true: Later is a figment of our very powerful imaginations. Now, truly, is all there is.)

It may sound funny, but the only way to experience enough right now is to actually participate in having enough right now. This means that you must practice. This practice is your apprenticeship. That is, the actual effort and sincere attention you pay to the moments, however brief, of enough right now will be your teachers. Unlike the learned woman in the story, you need not look for some master or expert elsewhere! You are she. Do you see how accepting your own expertise is, in itself, an exercise in enough right now? By learning to trust yourself, you are acknowledging that *you* are enough right now. And when else could you possibly be enough, if not right now? For right now is all there is and all there will ever be.

How powerful this is! By dwelling in enough right now, you are consciously choosing not to worry: "Will there be enough later?" This nagging worry is another trick that scarcity plays: namely, the creation of constant distress that there will not be enough later which encourages selfishness and stingy behavior.

Being stingy means holding back, conserving, hanging on to what little you have because you're worried that even that will be taken away. At the beginning of 2014, I was chatting with Alice, a cashier at my local grocery store, and I asked her, "What's one thing you'd like to accomplish this coming year?" She told me that she makes baby quilts and she wanted to start a business selling them. As the conversation ended, she said that she planned to open an Etsy account and to get started selling her quilts online.

A few weeks later, I ran into Alice again and asked her about her quilt shop on Etsy. She hadn't opened it, she said, because if she made more than $600, she'd have to pay taxes on her earnings. Huh? That's right: Alice was afraid to make any money because then a small percentage would be taken away. That's stingy: Instead of making something, she'd prefer to withhold her gifts from the world and make nothing at all. And that's exactly the sort of scenario that's common when scarcity's lies are taken to be truth—the anxiety and fear over not having enough later completely derails the generosity of enough right now.

This example also speaks to how powerful the myth of scarcity is and the stranglehold it has over our minds, our hearts, and our society. Do not be discouraged, however! The experience of enough right now is significantly more powerful than the myth of more time later and once you've tasted enough time now, you will gain greater strength and courage to pursue your subsequent apprenticeships and your mastery of the alchemy of time.

It is very difficult, if not impossible, to be calm, bold, and centered when you're stuck in the mindset of "more time later." Scarcity's powerful gravity will alway be pulling you off kilter and out of shape, giving you the feeling that you are in danger of failing or falling. As soon as you stop orbiting scarcity and explore the expansive space of enough right now, you're likely to notice a greater sense of confidence. This path of growing poise will contribute to feeling sexier. By trusting the now moment as the sacred space that it is, you will imbue your days with a spiritual quality that blesses every action you take.

WHAT WILL YOU PRACTICE IN YOUR APPRENTICESHIP TO ENOUGH?

Now, let's get down to brass tacks. Apprenticeships commonly begin with small tasks that, when performed with devotion and sincerity, earn the apprentice access to more complex knowledge and skills later on. In this apprenticeship to enough, you'll practice several skills and behaviors that, as they become second nature, provide the basis for mastery later on.

By trusting the now moment as the sacred space that it is, you will imbue your days with a spiritual quality that blesses every action you take.

- Because "more time later" incites procrastination and delay, you'll learn a deceptively simple technique for taking immediate action.

- After conquering procrastination, you'll gain the ability to start activities smoothly and to implement a smooth "ending" when you need to move on to another task. These skills reduce the friction that impairs your efficiency and wastes effort and energy.

- Because scarcity whispers that you don't have enough time to do your work now, you'll practice working in the time you do have available.

- Because there is enough time now, you'll learn the powerful technique of "shrinking work to fit."

Here are four tasks to get you started.

Task One: Taking Action Right Away

The first task in your apprenticeship to enough is taking action right away. To begin, you will practice the "Brief Daily Session." This deceptively simple method is insanely powerful for helping you to get started on any task and to dispel the notion that you must procrastinate or delay your work until you have "more time later," as the myth would counsel.

One of the reasons people end up procrastinating is resistance. I understand this feeling really well. Resistance is kin to fear: It's the feeling that I am not quite up to the challenge of what I'm longing to do. And resistance is not just associated with work that I loathe, like menu planning, bookkeeping, and dusting the furniture. I feel resistance when I want to make art, work in the garden, or spend time with people I love. Author Steven Pressfield writes, "The more important a call or action is to our soul's evolution, the more resistance we will feel toward pursuing it." In fact, Pressfield believes that resistance is so powerful that it can be a compass, pointing *toward* our yearnings, callings, and most important life's work.

To get around resistance anytime I'm stuck, I use my favorite technique: the "Brief Daily Session," or BDS, for short.

Tucking a BDS (or several) in your day is a painless way to get yourself started on something you really want (or need) to do but are hesitant to begin. Part of the lie scarcity whispers to fuel your resistance is that there isn't enough time to even start! The Brief Daily Session allows you to dispute this lie by beginning with ease and confidence.

*Resistance is kin to fear:
It's the feeling that you are not
quite up to the challenge of what
you're longing to do.*

The process is deceptively simple: Choose a short length of time (three to five minutes will do just fine), set a timer for your chosen BDS length, and start working on the thing you've been resisting. When your timer alarms, check in with yourself. Are you gathering momentum? If the timer hadn't interrupted you, would you still be working? If so, great! Keep going! Work until you reach completion or until you've used the time you had available.

But if you're not into the groove and still in the midst of resistance, note what you did by completing two sentences: 1) The last thing I did was... and 2) The next thing I'll do is... And you're done!

After her parents passed away, Margaret, one of my long-time clients, took responsibility for getting the family photos organized, scanned, and distributed to her siblings, nearly five thousand images in all. Using Brief Daily Sessions to get started each day, she sorted images, tossed those that were indistinct or blurry, identified people and places, and scanned them into the computer. Even though this was a project near and dear to her heart, Margaret often encountered resistance. "BDSs are the *only* way to tackle big, 'unending' projects," Margaret says. Her labor of love, which required hundreds of hours of work, wouldn't have been completed without Brief Daily Sessions, she explained. I've taught the Brief Daily Session to many, many people like Margaret, and everyone raves about how this technique helps them to get past resistance to do more of what they love from writing screenplays to starting Etsy stores. Why does the BDS approach work so well?

Brief Daily Sessions use the principle that "motivation follows involvement." Motivation doesn't suddenly come along for no reason, urging you into action. Resistance takes advantage of motivation's absence to discourage you from beginning and to woo you to wait until you have more motivation (and time) later. But motivation seems to follow involvement very reliably. That is, when you become engaged and attentive, even just a little bit, you'll start to feel a lessening of resistance and a sense that maybe, just maybe, you can do this.

Resistance, like its cousin scarcity, is a big fat liar: It tells you that tasks are bigger or harder to complete than they really are. BDSs whittle tasks down to itty bitty, bite-sized morsels. Five minutes is a piece of cake! And that allows you just enough of a toe-hold to call BS on resistance's lie. And often, that's enough to give you the experience of *enough time now.*

But the last reason that Brief Daily Sessions are effective is the biggest one: You learn to follow through on your intentions. The reason that procrastination is so insidious is it puts you in the habit of reneging on your intentions and breaking your promises to yourself. The key word is habit. Befriending procrastination means you're teaching yourself that you can't be relied upon. (You'll learn much more about reliability in a later chapter; the most important kind of reliability is your ability to make and keep promises to yourself.)

Being afraid or reluctant to start can leave you feeling timid, and timid is neither sexy nor soul-full! The Brief Daily Session is a lovely way to take a baby step toward the kind of boldness that is at the heart of being a Sexy + Soul-full woman. Each BDS is practice in taking action without concern for how something will turn out: If after three minutes, you're not feeling more motivation, so what? Three minutes of action is preferable to hours and hours of being stuck in resistance.

Beware of the trap of expecting to arrive at enough all at once—you won't. Residing in enough right now will occur gradually, as you continue perfecting your skills. The Brief Daily Session also allows you to advance in enough time now by gaining skill in starting and stopping work on demand—the second task in your apprenticeship.

Task Two: Starting and Stopping Work "On Demand"

How many times have you come to work on what you love and found yourself dithering around, feeling confused about what to do, or just having a hard time settling yourself? Too many, right? Starting work without all that fuss is a skill—a behavior that's learned and practiced—and it goes hand-in-glove with stopping work on demand; that is, wrapping up so you can move on to something else. These two skills, starting and stopping on demand, work in partnership to help you to get involved in doing more of what you love quickly and then to shift gears readily. Both are important in helping you learn to work in the time you have available (the third task in your apprenticeship) and, ultimately, in experiencing enough time now.

Paradoxically, starting on demand often springs from stopping well. This is where your first task, the Brief Daily Session, sets the stage for advancing your apprenticeship. You learn to start by slipping past resistance in a low-stakes, easy, and short little session that allows you to simply begin. Then, as you end your BDS, you make note of what to do next, using those two helpful sentences: "The last thing I did was..." and "The next thing I'll do is..." With this gentle ending, you lay the foundation for starting on demand when you return to your project the next time.

Starting on demand requires that you settle down and go to work right away. To do this successfully means preparing in advance as well as cultivating the mindset that you'll not tolerate any delay. The success of any apprenticeship comes from sincerity and devotion. The greater your sincerity and the more intense your devotion, the faster you'll progress in your mastery of the alchemy of time. Simply trust yourself and what you wrote as the last thing you did and the next thing you'll do. You had enough wisdom in that moment to complete those sentences; you were equal to the demands at hand. You have enough wisdom now, too! Lean into your trust and begin where you said you would. Like any acts of faith, leaning into trust and standing on wisdom is deep work which will contribute to your growth as a Sexy + Soul-full woman.

If you find that you're having trouble settling down, it's often because something else is on your mind—in that case, take five minutes to get clear. I am so often in my head that I forget I have a body! Clearing my mind is often a matter of reconnecting with my physical self by taking a walk, doing a few yoga poses, or stretching out on the floor to fully relax my back and open my chest. I often use writing to settle myself, too; I whip out my journal and let my thoughts pour out onto the page through my hand. Within moments, my mind is at ease, and I feel ready to begin my work, doing more of what I love.

A consciously soul-full approach is also very helpful to starting work on demand. Think of how you'd behave if you were invited to work in some holy place like a temple or meditation space. You'd quiet yourself before you entered and you'd gather everything you needed so you wouldn't dither about and disturb anyone with your confusion. You'd enter the workspace with reverence and respect, intent not just on getting your work done but also to demonstrate how much you care. That's the kind of attitude that, when brought to your daily tasks, will elevate them to touch the sacred. "Every moment," writes Sister Ruth Burrows, "is an opportunity for God to love us and for us to respond [to that] love." As I was writing this book, I made a short devotional prayer at the beginning of each work session. Each day, I lit a candle and asked the divine for help in finishing my book. By praying, I created a gentle entry point that helped me to calm myself and to start work on demand.

When you're feeling a great deal of urgency, taking the time to pray or to clear your thoughts may seem like a waste. In truth, however, these moments can make time feel more spacious! As you will learn in the next chapter, mindfulness is an important aspect of shaping your perception and experiences of time. In addition, the sincerity of your efforts in starting well will affirm your faith and trust in having enough time now. When I find myself feeling fearful, I remind myself that my fear is in conflict with my trust—I can't have both fear and trust at the same time. In that moment, I consciously choose to trust, and you can, too. Simply affirm trust, even when you don't "feel" as if it's true that there is enough time now. Only by experiencing enough, even in small and seemingly trivial ways, will you begin to learn that there is truly enough.

Remember what it is you're working toward: Doing more of what you love, with whom you love. When you bring that sense of anticipation to all of your work, it changes how you approach what you're doing. You're no longer having to force yourself to start the job and no longer dragging your feet about getting things done. Furthermore, wallowing in resistance only fuels the fires that scarcity uses to create urgency and fear. Enough! By encouraging your devotion and apprenticeship to enough time now, you can approach every task with love and generosity of spirit. Every

When you find yourself feeling fearful, remind yourself that your fear is in conflict with your trust—you can't have both fear and trust at the same time.

step you take brings you closer to what you love! By holding your love close to your heart as you do your daily work, you'll gain an energy as well as a joy that will nourish your spirit and move you forward. This is the mindset that will help you the most as you start your work right away and do your work now.

As you grow in your ability to start on demand, you'll ready yourself for the next task in your apprenticeship: Working in the time available.

TASK THREE: WORKING IN THE TIME AVAILABLE

Working in the time available is the art of doing what you can, with what you have, in the time you've got. Throughout every day, you will find yourself with a few extra minutes. You may be between appointments or waiting on someone to get ready to leave the house. Perhaps you've completed a project or a task. Or maybe you've set aside an hour for something close to your heart: the novel you've been aching to write, the collage of your big vision for the coming year, or capturing more lines of the play you've been penning.

It would be wonderful, yes, to be on sabbatical with days and days of unbroken hours to dedicate to your loves (or to any of the other work you do). But sadly, the sabbatical experience isn't common. Dribs and drabs of moments, however, are freely available and in abundance. Or to put it another way, there is enough time now. Enough time now to make progress, move forward, and experience the joys of doing more of what you love.

Writers seem especially prone to getting caught up in thinking that they need large blocks of undisturbed time to complete their masterworks. But when novelist Susan Strait began her first book, she was a young mother—she didn't have the luxury of child care or time to herself—so she wrote her book by using "found" moments throughout the day. She wrote on street corners, while waiting for the light to change. She wrote in the car, sitting in the parking lot when she had a few extra minutes before work. She wrote everywhere and anywhere, on just about any scrap of paper that would hold words: receipts, subscription cards from magazines, the backs of grocery lists. Even now, years later, she still writes this way, capturing scenes and bits of dialog wherever she goes. She's mastered working in the time available and doing more of what she loves through dedication and practice. And so you can, too.

Your loves may not be portable but there are ways of taking them with you everywhere to stimulate your creativity and to be in close proximity to your love. One of the ways I accomplish doing more of what I love is by cultivating my powers of observation. I am crazy about making mosaics and I am always on the look out for little bits of glass or other items that can be incorporated into my artwork. Everywhere I go, I find inspiration for mosaic, from the way the stones are fitted together in a sidewalk to how the mechanics of my local auto shop stacked old tires into a shipping crate. Working on noticing is one of the ways you can practice the art of doing more of what you love in the time available.

You can easily see how the first tasks of your apprenticeship serve you in this undertaking of working in the time available. You have already begun starting work right away by doing Brief Daily Sessions and practicing starting and stopping work on demand. You elevate these skills to another level as you apply them to working in the time available.

{WHEN YOU have a few unscheduled minutes, ask yourself, "What can I do in the time I have now?" Maybe it's a phone call or dusting your desk. Perhaps it's filling out a form you've been resisting (using a Brief Daily Session to get going, perhaps). By keeping a well-curated task list, you can find any number of items waiting for your attention that can be dispatched during time you have available.}

Often, we waste these extra moments throughout the day. When I'm not at my best, I find myself wanting to use those spaces in my schedule to check email or peep at Instagram. But if I'm honest with myself, there is enough time to get all sorts of essential, yet small tasks completed. When I work in the time I have available, the doing gets me clearer and nearer to doing more of what I love. So ask yourself: Would you rather get lost in Facebook or check off some task that will allow you to leave your job a few minutes earlier?

I was waiting for a prescription at the local clinic's pharmacy recently and met a soul-full productivity sister who was making the most of working in the time available. Over the drone of voices in the atrium of the building, I heard the distinctive hum of a sewing machine. I followed the sound to the espresso kiosk (yes, I live in the Pacific Northwest, where you can get a fancy coffee drink practically anywhere). At the kiosk, I found the barista who, between customers, was piecing quilts. She exercises her creativity and shares her love of pattern and color with passersby, pausing to make a latte when a customer arrives. What a fabulous example of working in the time available and doing more of what you love! Granted, not everyone can take a sewing machine to their desk, but slipping a little sketchbook into your purse for drawing during a break, using your phone's camera to capture inspiration on the fly, scribbling a few lines of poetry or drafting a bit of dialog during your break—all are easily accessible ways to do more of what you love by working in the time available.

The more you practice this discipline of noticing when there is enough time now and using those spaces wisely, the more confident you will become in your ability to do more of what you love. Whenever you sense that growing confidence, savor the feeling—take it into your body and your soul. Now you're ready to harness that self-assurance in learning the last and most advanced task in your apprenticeship to enough: Shrinking work to fit.

TASK FOUR: SHRINKING WORK TO FIT

The fourth, and last, task in your apprenticeship to enough is a more advanced practice of working with the time available called "shrink to fit." By practicing shrink to fit, you will begin morphing tasks down to size to fit in the time you have available to do them. This magic trick makes use of what you learned as you practiced taking action right away, starting on demand, and working in the time available. Now, you will add a powerful new skill that is deeply rooted in fierce trust of enough.

Shrink to fit is especially useful in conquering obstacles that get between you and your loves. You already know that work has the amazing ability to expand and overflow if you give it no boundaries, yes? Shrink to fit plays on exactly that principle, but in reverse. Instead of giving tasks free rein and doggedly working until they're finished, shrink to fit sets a limit on how much effort you'll expend. In other words, you shrink the work to fit the time available, thus making enough time now.

Here's an example of how powerful shrink to fit can be. A friend of mine—a woman of enormous prestige and influence in biology—was working on her book, a tome that eventually weighed in at over 700 pages. One of her colleagues read and commented on every single chapter. "He was the only person who read the book in its entirety before it was published," she told me.

This colleague of hers was an incredibly accomplished professor with many graduate students, he carried a substantial teaching load, and, at the same time, he was very engaged with both his family and his community. He returned drafts to her so quickly and so reliably (unlike her other reviewers; sadly, one of whom was me), that she became curious as to how he was pulling the feat off.

When she asked him what the magic was, he explained that he decided in advance exactly how much time he was going to devote to reading her manuscript and then, when each chapter arrived, he simply blocked out that amount of time to complete his review in the time he made available. His feedback, she told me, was always thoughtful and germane. It was clear that he hadn't hurried—he'd actually carefully read and thought about what she'd written. This is precisely the power of shrink to fit, in service of *enough time now.*

To put the secret in shrinking work to fit in your own life, you must learn to recognize enough when you see it. Learning to spot enough takes some practice but probably less effort than you might think. This is really an exercise in identifying the most essential elements of getting something done and then doing just that—enough—with nothing added. This is also the path to becoming a "good-enoughist."

To be a good-enoughist, you decide the minimum level of quality that you're comfortable with and then aim for that. If you're a perfectionist, becoming a good-enoughist will require, little by little, letting go of seeking perfection and accepting some flaws. Scarcity will always attempt to convince you that perfection is required to have some chance of reaching enough. You know by now (I hope!), that scarcity is lying to you.

There is a point of "good enough" in every single task, project, and undertaking. Good enough is not a sloppy, one-size-fits-all quality. For some projects, good enough is very simple and, even, at times, mediocre is a perfectly acceptable outcome. On other occasions, good enough must meet a very high standard of excellence and elegance. When determining just how good "good enough" is for a certain task or project, you must trust in your own ability and expertise. Rely on your wisdom and experience to ascertain what good enough is for each situation. If you are a recovering perfectionist, take your first estimate of good enough and then aim one step lower. That small step will give you the breathing space to begin approaching good enough without quite so much anxiety. Then you can begin to trust and embrace your ability to let go of the need to endlessly pursue perfect, and you can begin to experience the joy of good enough.

Many times, what causes a task to exceed good enough is adding too much value. That is, we do more than we actually must do—we add flourishes and embellishments.

Some years ago, I was on a scholarship awards committee. The committee's job was to review applications and to find the five best applications. That was all. One member of the committee took this to mean: Read each application to the finest detail, create a detailed spreadsheet to track all aspects of each proposal, and compare every single candidate according to each category.

So how did I handle the review process? I made one pass to weed out the applicants that were either clearly unqualified or those who hadn't supplied all the requested information (often, reading the first paragraph was sufficient). I made a second pass to find the applications that stood out as being the best written. I made a third pass to read in detail that handful of the highest quality applications and rank them. I took the top five of those and that was that. I trusted my expertise and background as enough to make good decisions. And guess what? My "good enough" rankings weren't any different from the person who spent much more time painstakingly comparing every applicant.

Once you have determined what good enough is, you'll need to be focused on the work at hand. Decide how much time and energy you are willing to allot to this matter. Engage with the other skills of enough time now: Take action right away, start and stop on demand, and work in the time available. Screen out distractions and hold off interruptions, too. Suffice it to say that to have the greatest success with shrink to fit, work with alacrity. Be decisive and succinct.

{ANOTHER WAY of approaching shrink to fit is to use the Pomodoro technique. Created by an Italian software programmer, Francesco Cirillo, and named after the tomato shaped kitchen timer he used (*pomodoro* is Italian for "tomato"), the Pomodoro technique teaches you to work in twenty-five minute bouts. (Each twenty-five minute session is one "Pomodoro.") Here's how it works: You set a timer for twenty-five minutes and start work on demand. When the timer elapses, you stop on demand and take a five minute break by getting up to stretch, grabbing a bathroom break, or getting a glass of water. After five minutes, you go right back to work.

After four "Pomodoros," you take a longer break of fifteen minutes or so. I use a timer app on my iPhone that allows me to program different alarm sounds and even a nice, soothing grandfather clock ticking sound that helps me stay focused during a twenty-five minute work bout. This method encourages intense focus for short bouts, just exactly what's needed for shrink to fit, as well as a sustainable rhythm of effort and rest.}

The most important points to remember about shrink to fit are:

- Identify, in advance, what good enough is for the finished product.

- Estimate how much time is needed to complete the task by reaching good enough.

- Work intensely, with concentration, to finish in the time allotted.

Because shrink to fit is an advanced skill, you will need quite a lot of practice to get really good at it. At first, you are likely to over- or under-estimate how much time you really need. Keep a journal and track your efforts. You'll quickly learn how much time tasks really take. You may also have trouble with spotting what is good enough. If you're recovering from perfectionism, pay attention to cues about how people respond to your gentle efforts at good enough versus your usual no-effort-is-too-much approaches.

Finally, you may discover that you're highly distractible or that your environment is very interruption-prone. In the next chapter, you'll be apprenticed to ease, and your first task includes mindfulness, a practice that will help you to stay on task more reliably.

To be a Sexy + Soul-fully productive woman, you need to produce. Producing means completion. Completion increases confidence and, besides, it feels incredible! The better you get at shrink to fit, the more you will finish and the more freedom you'll gain to do more of what you love.

SUMMARY

Here's a quick summary of the tasks in your apprenticeship to enough.

Task One: Learn to take action right away by using Brief Daily Sessions.

- Set your timer for three to five minutes.
- Dive right in and work until your timer alarms.
  - >If motivation follows involvement, keep going!
  - >Not feeling it? Wrap up.
- When you stop working, complete two sentences:
  - >The last thing I did was...
  - >The next thing I'll do is...

Task Two: Master starting and stopping on demand.

- Set the stage by using a Brief Daily Session and completing the two sentences at the end as above.
- Practice trust and begin where you said you would.
- If you're having trouble settling down, try:
  - >Taking a short walk to work off excessive energy.
  - >Making a list quickly of what's bothering you.
  - >Praying or meditating to calm yourself.

Task Three: Working in the time available.

- Find ways to take what you love with you, wherever you go.
- Keep a well-curated task list so you can easily answer the

question: What can I get done in the few minutes available?

- Take advantage of creative opportunities which show up at times or places you don't expect by having tools, like your phone's camera, a sketchbook, or a journal, with you.

Task Four: Shrinking work to fit.

- Decide how much time to allot to the task at hand.
- Identify what "good enough" is and what you need to do to get there.
- Tackle your work with gusto.
- Try the Pomodoro Technique to work in intense, focused bouts.

By practicing these tasks—taking action right away, starting and stopping work on demand, working in the time available, and shrinking work to fit—you will gain valuable experience with enough time now. You will see your efforts bear fruit as you do more than you thought you were capable of. Simultaneously, you are generating your own proof that you do truly have enough time now, enabling you to reject the myth of "more time later" once and for all.

Once you reject this first myth, you've taken an important step towards mastering the alchemy of time. Your next apprenticeship will allow you to reject the myth that time is outside your control.

chapter six

Time Is What I Think It Is: An Apprenticeship to Ease

IN THE LAST chapter, we discarded the first myth about time and practiced four skills to give you enough time now.

Let's move on to second in our three destructive myths about time: "Time is outside my control." That myth is about to undergo a metamorphosis into a much lovelier and far more helpful truth about time: "Time is what I think it is."

While it is certainly true that the clock and its inexorable tick-tick-tick is beyond anyone's ability to stop, stall, speed, or alter, your perception of time is entirely yours. We will use some surprisingly simple and seemingly ordinary methods to give you practice in sculpting and molding time: tailoring it to fit you like a haute couture ball gown that a Hollywood starlet might wear on the red carpet.

What Does it Mean to Be Apprenticed to Ease?

For years, I labored under the delusion that ease was a synonym for lazy. My misperception was rooted in my addiction to doing, and I was distinctly hostile toward anything that smacked of ease. As a result, I looked down on anyone or anything that advocated stillness, rest, or play. "...There's a kind of misperception and dis-ease [sic] which filters into our character whereby we start to cultivate a kind of arrogance that we're the only ones who are players," says poet David Whyte. "We're the only ones who are doing the work, and others are somehow out on the periphery and not participating and don't deserve to be a part of any rewards, which are naturally given to a human being who's been good and done their work and fulfilled their duties."

David's wise words describe exactly how I used to feel about ease when I was stuck in the myth "Time is outside my control." I felt trapped in a rat race against the clock. By running faster and faster, I convinced myself that I was winning, or if not winning, still somehow superior to people who moved at a slower pace than I did.

Yet now, my perspective is entirely reversed. So how did I achieve this turn-around and begin to value ease so highly that I'd apprentice you to it? I learned that ease means freedom.

When well-versed in ease, you are free to choose the kind of relationship with time you want to have.

When well-versed in ease, you are free to choose the kind of relationship with time you want to have. Your pace is no longer dictated to you by the clock or by urgency, and you become free to operate from the knowledge that time is what you think and say it is. Using a more deliberate, conscious approach, you're able to choose your experience. By operating from a more heartfelt, centered, Sexy + Soul-full vantage point, you can opt out of urgency to choose a relaxed and alert mindset instead.

A word of caution, however. If you cannot, even for a moment, release your grasp on your list of tasks and projects, or if you're unable to unplug from ceaseless inputs like your phone or social media, then the apprenticeship to ease may prove difficult for you. The door to this path of mastery might be hard to open, but it will budge. By remaining devoted to the first apprenticeship to enough, you will eventually have plenty of confidence to proceed to the next stage of your apprenticeship—to learn to gain control of your mind, not of time, so you can say with certainty, "Time is what I think it is."

WHAT WILL YOU PRACTICE IN YOUR APPRENTICESHIP TO EASE?

When you are ready to proceed, your apprenticeship to ease will consist of four tasks.

- You will learn time "shape shifting" skills by practicing mindfulness.

- You will alter your perception by changing how you talk about time.

- You will declare independence from the clock by creating a clearing in your schedule.

- You will enjoy your new-found freedom by honoring stillness.

TASK ONE: SHAPE TIME BY PRACTICING MINDFULNESS

The first task in your apprenticeship to ease is to shape time by practicing mindfulness. Mindfulness can be defined and taught in many ways. In this early part of your apprenticeship, I will

By operating from a more heartfelt, centered, Sexy + Soul-full vantage point, you can opt out of urgency to choose a relaxed and alert mindset instead.

ask you to practice a simple form of mindfulness: just noticing details of the world around you.

Our brains use the presence of fine details (or lack of them) as an indicator of how fast time is passing. When we move faster in an effort to keep pace with an ever more complex world, life seems to go by in a blur. As we observe fewer details, the brain assumes that time is going by quickly. When the brain captures more detailed information about the world, it assumes that time is passing more slowly. This simple distinction about details is the key to begin shifting the shape of time from quite small and cramped to more spacious and roomy.

To notice details is quite easy. Wherever you are, take a breath and cultivate awareness of the sensation of your breath as it passes through your nose. Do this right now. Just one mindful breath: in....and out. Nothing is as close to you as your breath. It's with you at all times and it's always available to provide an anchor for your attention to details.

Your only duty for the first few days of your apprenticeship to ease is: Notice your breath. Whenever you happen to think about it, bring your attention to your breath for one inhalation and a slow exhalation, which takes only a few seconds at most. No one will notice that you're mindfully taking a breath. To help encourage your awareness, you can set a reminder for yourself on your calendar or smartphone or identify a marker in your environment. For example, as you're leaving your apartment, you can chant: "When I see my train, I'll think of my breath." And lo, as you're standing on the platform watching your train come in, you'll remember to notice the details of your breath.

This practice of breath-noticing will have several effects. Right away, you will feel a bit calmer and any urgency you may be experiencing will feel less intense. Physiologically, a deep breath both slows your heart rate and decreases your blood pressure. In turn, these relaxation responses turn down the heat of stress, leaving you with a sense of peace. Second, you will gain sensitivity to smaller and smaller nuances. At first, the details of your breath will be quite broad and perhaps only intellectual. With practice, your body will supply you with more information, and you'll begin to notice richer textures, such as the coolness in your nostrils on the inhale, how air temperature changes between your nostrils and your throat, the expansion of your chest, and so on. The more you notice, the more there will be to notice! In addition, you will be creating a centering point.

Centering is one of the doorways to ease and the beginning of real freedom—a freedom that comes from inside you and that is fully yours. It is a sense of self-possession and internal comfort that will grow in scope as your apprenticeship in ease continues. As I've mentioned before, being centered is a key quality of the Sexy + Soul-full woman, and attending to your breath is a simple yet especially effective way to transition to this state of being.

By cultivating mindfulness through your breath, you get out of your head and into your body, integrating the physical with the intellectual. Simultaneously, attending to your breath can become a pivotal spiritual practice. "Every breath can be a doorway to awareness and awakening. This is why attending to one's breath is such a foundational spiritual practice," writes psychologist and spiritual teacher, David Benner. "... Each breath we receive is a gift of God, drawing God into our very being. Attending to our breathing is, therefore, a prayerful way of opening our selves to God—an opening that can be an awakening." Simply put, prayerfully noticing your breath helps you to become more Soul-full.

When you become skilled at noticing the finer details of your breath, you can turn your attention to noticing more details in the world around you. Add noticing odors to the landscape of your breath. Cultivate your awareness of temperature on your skin. Feel the weight of your body on your buttocks when you sit or your feet when you stand. Notice the sidewalk under your feet, symbols on signs, or colors of clothing. While you're noticing, simply gaze. There is no need to ask yourself what something means or whether you are reminded of something else. Just notice.

You can do this at any moment of the day, but be especially aware of practicing this kind of noticing when you feel time pressure. When you catch yourself feeling rushed or overwhelmed, notice the details around you: Your breath, bodily sensations, the environment around you. These details are the source of your brain's perception of time. The more details you are able to gather, the better! Your brain will respond by slowing down the pace of your perception of time, even if only a tiny bit, granting you some ease.

However, don't look for results just yet. Stay focused on noticing the details and cultivating mindfulness. Your ability to connect with your breath and gather more details from your experiences will continue to grow as you take on the second task of your apprenticeship to ease: changing your perception of time by altering what you say.

TASK TWO: ALTER YOUR PERCEPTION OF TIME BY CHANGING YOUR LANGUAGE

"Time is a created thing," wrote philosopher Lao Tzu, "To say 'I don't have time,' is like saying 'I don't want to.'"

Your language—how you express your thoughts—is one of the most powerful ways you create your perception of time. Whatever it is that you say about your time is true for you. Like Alicia, the client I described earlier in the book, you may be using all sorts of phrases, almost a litany of sorts, to reinforce your feelings of being rushed, running out of time, and being unable to keep up with the too-fast pace of life.

Modern neuroscience backs up what Lao Tzu surmised over two thousand years ago. Time is a "created thing," manufactured by your brain as a way to make sense of the world. "The days of thinking of time as a river—evenly flowing, always advancing—are over," says David Eagleman. "Time perception, just like vision, is a construction of the brain..."

Rather than go into a detailed explanation of how your brain creates your experience of time, the main thing I want you to remember is your brain is incredibly powerful—so powerful that it can convince you that the flow of time has been altered. To turn this miraculous ability of your brain to your advantage, you need to change the way you talk about your time.

Don't forget: Your perception about your situation is the reality you live in. If you believe that you're running out of time, that's true for you. And the more you say it, the more convinced you'll be. "Beliefs are mental objects in the sense that they are embedded in the brain," says neuroscientist, Kathleen Taylor. "If you challenge [beliefs] by contradiction, ...then they are going to weaken slightly. If that is combined with very strong reinforcement of new beliefs, then you're going to get a shift in emphasis from one to the other." By changing your language, while continuing to practice the skills of your first apprenticeship, you can create new beliefs about time, which then alter your perception of reality, exchanging a rushed and frantic lifestyle for one that is less hectic and more sustainable.

You can create new beliefs about time, exchanging a rushed frantic lifestyle for one that is less hectic & more sustainable.

In your first task, you practiced noticing your breath. In this task, you'll begin by noticing what you say out loud or think to yourself about time. At first, you'll just listen for the word "time." When you catch yourself talking or thinking about time, notice exactly what you've said. What perception are you perpetuating in your language? Then ask: What reality would you prefer over the one you're currently speaking about?

Once you've gotten pretty good at hearing yourself talk about time, decide how you'd like to change your language. Taking greater responsibility for your language about time will also help prepare you for another important skill: Saying 'no' with love and courage.

SAYING "NO" WITH LOVE AND COURAGE

One of the most valuable skills you can ever acquire is the ability to say "no" without squirming, apologizing, bargaining, or making excuses. Saying "no" often feels very uncomfortable and many people are hesitant to risk making someone else angry or unhappy. Yet, a reluctant "yes" can wreak as much or more havoc than a well-spoken "no." Here's how to go about learning the skill of saying "no" with love and courage.

- Find the space between request and response. Using the skill of mindfulness, begin noticing requests and practice finding the moment between the request and your response. The more attention you pay to this space, the more room you will have to make a conscious, well considered decision rather than blurting out, "Yes!"

- Give yourself permission to feel your discomfort about saying "no" without giving into it. The discomfort is a normal response to a potentially uncomfortable situation. However, discomfort about saying "no" isn't a good enough reason to say "yes" instead.

- Allow yourself to feel tenderness toward the person or opportunity you are saying "no" to. Anger or ill feelings can be a natural reaction in situations when one or both people are unhappy. Reassure yourself that saying "no" isn't an act of ill will, it's a brave and truthful answer.

- Stand your ground. Brené Brown's mantra is, "Don't shrink, don't puff up, stand your sacred ground." You can make her mantra your own or come up with your own phrase that helps you to remain courageous in the face of opposition to your no. If your response was well-considered and you're certain that no was the right answer, stick with it. Remember: Backing off of your "no" could teach someone a lesson about you that you'd rather they not learn.

Changing your perception of time isn't just about your language, it's also about your willingness to allocate time as a resource. Recently, someone at church invited me to join a six-week study group. Rather than repeating the rote answer "I don't have time," what I said was, "That commitment doesn't fit with my schedule." My answer was based on my understanding that a) I create my perception of time by how I talk about it and b) I am in control of how I make use of time. By acknowledging that I allocate time through my schedule, I gave an honest answer that didn't include reinforcing the notion that "I don't have time." The truth is there is enough time—for what I've already committed to undertake.

{You might want to write down your stock phrases about time–the ones you want to stop using–and draft new ways of talking about time.

- "I'm running out of time" might become "I know how to work in the time I have available" (and you do, thanks to your work in your first apprenticeship to enough time now).

- "I don't have time to finish this" might turn into "I can shrink this work to fit the time available."

- If you find yourself saying, "Time is going by too quickly," you can say, "I know how to slow time's pace by attending to details," and then tune into the nuances of your breath.}

Since I've been working on increasing my sensitivity to how I talk to myself about time, I've noticed many changes in how I feel. One of the most helpful differences is reducing the anxiety I experience. When I find myself starting to feel worried about time, I carefully choose words that reflect how I want to feel about time. Just this morning, when I was getting anxious about completing all the tasks I had in front of me, I reminded myself, "I have time for a good breakfast," and I sat on the porch and savored the flavor of fresh peaches, the crunch of almonds, and the tangy taste of fresh yogurt. Those details, along with my words, helped me to shape my perception of time as more spacious.

With your practice in altering time by changing your language of it, you're now ready to take a much bolder step in your apprenticeship: declaring your independence from the clock.

Task Three: Declare Independence from the Clock by Creating a Clearing in Your Schedule

One of the results of mindfulness is a sense of greater interior freedom. Some spiritual writers refer to this phenomenon as a healthy sense of detachment. You'll explore this kind of detachment in greater depth when you reach your apprenticeship to equanimity in the following chapter. For now, however, you'll enhance your experience of interior freedom by making a more outward declaration of independence as you clear some space in your schedule to escape the tyranny of the clock.

When you practiced your apprenticeship to enough right now, you worked with your existing schedule. This was necessary for two reasons: One, you must start where you are, and two, you had to gain experience in enough to reject the myth of "more time later."

Now that you've kicked the first myth to the curb, you'll work with your future time in a more conscious and effective way as you continue to do away with myth number two. The goal for this task is to experience the freedom of being "off the clock." You'll gain the ability to stop keeping a vigil of the hours and to be totally in the moment.

Try to remember the last time you felt so at ease that you didn't know what time it was and didn't care. This kind of freedom is so rare in modern life that you may not have experienced it in many years—maybe not even since childhood!

I know freedom from the clock may sound like a fantasy but I assure you it's real. You can truly experience this emancipation but first, you must exert your ability to clear space in your schedule.

EXERCISE:

To clear some space for yourself, scroll ahead in your calendar. Eventually, sometime in the weeks and months ahead, you will come to the boundary of scheduled and not-yet-scheduled. Regard your calendar, gaze at this boundary, and focus on your breath. Find your center, as you've been doing during your first task of shaping time through mindfulness. Then look into this spacious landscape of the not-yet-scheduled and find a parcel of it to call your own. Maybe it's a Sunday afternoon when your beloved will be distracted by basketball playoffs. Perhaps it's a morning before an out-of-office appointment or a Friday before a Monday holiday.

When you see this morsel of time, allocate the space in your schedule as your own. Yes, right now, before you lose your nerve or talk yourself out of it, block out on your calendar the space of time in minutes and hours that will be yours and yours alone. If you need to make some arrangements, like for childcare or requesting time off from work, make note of those in your task list and take care of them right away. Do not procrastinate. Like enough right now, this freedom must be experienced to be understood and grasped. There is no surrogate or proxy.

When your space, the time that you've owned as yours comes

around, set the alarm on your phone to notify you when you must go back on the clock. And then...stop looking at the time until your alarm sounds.

The first time I tasted the freedom of being off the clock, I found myself feeling worried. What time was it? How much time do I have left? These worries are so deeply ingrained in us that letting go of them is hard. In fact, releasing those concerns felt a little risky! Once I began to trust the safety net of my alarm, I realized that I had nothing to fret about and a new sort of peace and joy descended over me. Gone was the need to constantly race the clock: I could simply be. Be wherever I was, doing whatever I was doing. The freedom was completely intoxicating! And in combination with mindfulness of the details around me, the time stretched, grew, and felt even more luxurious and spacious.

{ALMOST AS soon as you create a clearing in your schedule, you may begin to experience pressure to give that space away. The pressure you feel may come from inside, like a little gremlin whispering, "Who do you think you are to give yourself this kind of freedom?" Alternatively, the duress may be from people around you, albeit innocently, as they make requests or place demands on your schedule. In a later chapter, you'll learn more about making and keeping promises to yourself but in the meantime, here are a few helpful hints about resisting the temptation to pave over your clearing with other commitments.

- Coin a standard response that is truthful but not too self-disclosing. When someone asks for an appointment on a day that I have set aside for myself, I say, "I'm not available then."

- Color code the space in your calendar to help you see the clearing as a real commitment. Often, our appointments with ourselves are treated as imaginary or ephemeral, as if they lack real substance. At first, you may need to create a name or a code word to make your space into reality. Many women are very accustomed to putting everyone and everything else ahead of themselves. When putting yourself first by creating a clearing in your schedule, you may encounter uncomfortable feelings. The key to overcoming these barriers is to notice and to name the feelings when they arise. Breathe. Reply to the feelings with compassion and calm. You can use a mantra like, "I have a right to space in my own calendar," or "This clearing is important to my wellbeing," or make up one of your own! Post your mantra where you can see it often to engrave it on your heart and mind.}

What will you do in this clearing that is yours? Lavish your freedom on what you love! Find a coffee shop and read a novel (it's incredible how decadent that feels!). Visit a local art museum. Take a long walk through a neighborhood you've always wanted to explore. Go to the library and browse the books on a subject you've wanted to learn more about. If you're an artist, make art. If you're a quilter, play with fabric. And while you're enjoying your love(s), be very aware of all the details. The more richly experienced and more deeply engaged you are, the more your brain will reward you with slowing down the perceived pace of your time.

If you're able to fully immerse yourself in your freedom from the clock, you may even experience a state of flow. Flow is a mental state that occurs when your concentration is very intensely focused. When you're in a state of flow, time seems to stand still and, paradoxically, hours can seem like minutes. Often, when I experience flow, I feel that time doesn't exist at all. You will luxuriate in this feeling, trust me.

> *Busyness is a way of avoiding stillness, which is the ultimate expression of ease.*

Reveling in your freedom from the clock is especially rewarding in terms of growing as a Sexy + Soul-fully productive woman. When you are off the clock, you are free to be rather than to do. Putting your focus on being connects you with your authentic self. As this connection deepens, you'll learn more about who you are. St. Teresa of Avila explains the importance of self knowledge this way: "No matter how high a state the soul attains, she can never neglect knowing herself... Fears arise from not knowing ourselves. Fear distorts the knowledge of the self."

Of course, even one experience of this freedom is nice. However, apprenticeships are exercises in repeated practice. So after you've had one experience of being off the clock, go right back to your calendar and plan your next session by creating another clearing. As you clear this space on your calendar, remind yourself that time is what you think it is. If you think of time as spacious and roomy, you'll treat it differently than if you continue to think of time as outside your control.

Now you are ready to enter the final phase of your apprenticeship to ease and take on the last task: honoring stillness.

TASK FOUR: ENHANCE YOUR FREEDOM BY HONORING STILLNESS

With the experience of freedom and the growing ability to alter your perception of time, you will ready yourself for the most advanced task in your apprenticeship to ease: Honoring stillness.

Some psychologists believe that our ability to allow our minds to wander and get lost in our own thoughts is the basis of both empathy and creativity.

If you were to take a moment, remain motionless, and focus on your breathing, you might be able to hold still for a few moments—or, you might find yourself craving the distraction of your smart phone, Facebook, Twitter, or whatever else it is that you use to keep yourself amused. The other day, I watched a young woman while she walked down a hotel hallway, her face illuminated by the sickly green glow emitted by her phone. She got into the elevator with me, and I saw that she was playing a game. She was almost zombie-like; I found myself wondering what would happen if she had to be without her digital pacifier. Based on the research findings, she'd probably prefer to zap herself with a taser than give up her phone.

A recent study into the experience of stillness asked participants to remain in silent thought for 6 to 15 minutes. Most of the men (64%) and a few of the women (only 15%) preferred to administer painful electric shocks to themselves rather than be alone in their own heads. The majority of the participants, both men and women, described being still and alone in thought, with no distractions, as a negative experience.

Busyness is a way of avoiding stillness, which is the ultimate expression of ease. Being immersed in busyness or being addicted to digital devices not only derails stillness but these distractions also have a very weird way of making time pass unusually quickly. One of my clients struggled with being late for appointments. Her problem wasn't a failure to prepare to leave early enough. Her problem was that when she got ready and saw she had a few spare minutes, she'd become anxious to fill the time and used a game to distract herself from her discomfort. Suddenly, the extra minutes were gone, and quite a few more besides!

Stillness is much too important to be avoided, however. The ability to be alone with your thoughts is considered essential to healthy human functioning. Some psychologists believe that our ability to allow our minds to wander and get lost in our own thoughts is the basis of both empathy and creativity. Without introspection, reflection, and insight, it's almost impossible to understand ourselves. "There is something in a person that sits and waits for the sound of the genuine in herself," said civil rights leader and theologian, Howard Thurman, "I wonder if you can get still enough—not quiet—still enough to hear rumbling up from your unique and essential idiom, the sound of the genuine in you. I don't know if you can, but this is your assignment."

This sound of the genuine is your own most authentic voice. The deepest, most sacred part of you, the sound of which is constantly drowned out by all the noise—from within and without. The sound of the genuine is the true guide of your soul, your soul-full wisdom, that you can only access when you honor stillness. From the perspective of the sacred, the Divine speaks to us in a "still, small voice," one we can only hear in the silence of our hearts.

Unlike *working* in the time available, a task you undertook in your apprenticeship to enough time now, in your apprenticeship to ease, you'll practice *being still* in the time available. Your task is to notice spaces in your day when stillness is offered to you. To accept the invitation of stillness, simply return to your breath, just as you did in the first task of this apprenticeship to ease. This morning, for example, while I was making my coffee, I practiced this task. As the espresso machine was humming away, I stood nearby, with my eyes closed, just feeling my breath—

Burnout can be easily prevented by taking time for stillness, rest, and play.

in and out. A few seconds later, almost involuntarily, I found myself reaching for my phone!

Because the tendency to veer away from stillness using digital distraction is so common, I suggest you consider fasting now and then. Fasting is a time-honored spiritual practice, most often consisting of eating less or skipping meals. In this case, I am suggesting you fast from distraction. If you're used to walking with headphones, go without them. If you're used to having music during your yoga practice, turn it off. If you're fond of Facebook, Instagram, Pinterest, or CandyCrush, delete the apps from your smartphone (don't worry, you can always put them back later). To enact your fast, choose its length: a day, an hour, a week. During your fast, each time you find yourself craving the distraction of what you're fasting from, choose stillness instead.

I began such a fast while I was writing this chapter. At first, my intention was to refrain from social media for seven days. However, after two weeks had passed, I was still fasting. One of the side effects I observed was that I started putting down my smartphone and no longer caring where I left it. Hours would go by and I'd realize that I wasn't craving the entertainment offered by some app. I became more and more comfortable without my phone's companionship and found stillness easier and easier to locate and enjoy. My time of fasting felt much more spacious and rich; I was less hurried and calmer than before.

How does this simple practice of stillness benefit your apprenticeship to ease? When you have mastered ease, you will enjoy a more spacious existence. Rather than mindlessly filling your days with doing, you have the option of being instead. As you allow yourself to just be, your relationship with the clock is greatly altered. Time becomes much more malleable. The tight, cramped quality of time you may be used to will give way to an openness. Your experiences will become richer and more fully textured, allowing you to enjoy the details which, as you know, are part of how your brain creates your perception of time. With stillness, you'll be more present and available to enjoy your freedom from the clock, extending the work you began earlier in this chapter.

Finally, you can use stillness as a doorway to rest and play. All too often, rest is considered an afterthought but it is impossible to be Sexy + Soul-full when you're exhausted! Speaking from experience, chronic exhaustion sets the stage for burnout—the loss of enthusiasm and vitality caused by overwork. Burnout can be easily prevented, however, by taking time for stillness, rest, and play.

Using the same approach as declaring independence from the clock, set aside time for real rest or to engage in play. These are activities that result in no accomplishments; they are recharging and replenishing instead. I always know when I'm not getting enough of these because I find myself feeling dry and listless. Sometimes all I need is a few minutes laying in the hammock on our deck to restore my energetic spark. Staring into space, letting my mind wander for a few minutes, often gives me just the respite I need to revive my creativity. My husband, Douglas, takes play breaks with our dog. He and the pup enjoy a round of fetch, which refreshes them both.

Having great comfort with stillness requires quite a lot of practice. Be gentle with yourself. As you grow in your ability to remain still, you'll be rewarded in unexpected ways. Your intuition, for example, may speak up when you most need its guidance. Your creativity will reward you with more ideas. Your energy will improve and your sense of contentment is likely to increase, as well. Most of all, you'll experience ease and the confidence in knowing "time is what you think it is."

SUMMARY

During your apprenticeship to ease, you've undertaken four important tasks. Here's a brief summary of each.

Task One: Shape time by practicing mindful attention to detail.

- Begin by noticing your breath. Whenever you happen to think about it, bring your attention to your breath for one inhalation followed by a slow exhalation.

- After a few days of cultivating awareness of your breath, cultivate an awareness of the details of your breath—the sensations in your throat and chest as you inhale and exhale.

- Practice noticing details of the world around you, especially when you feel pressured for time. Take a mindful breath and then observe your surroundings and sensations, noting as many details as you can.

Task Two: Alter your perception of time by changing your language.

- Notice what you say to yourself or to others about time. What words do you use? How do you describe your relationship with time?

- Write down the stock, habitual phrases you use about time. Now, transform those into sentences that accurately reflect the new perception about time you want to cultivate.

- Each time you catch yourself using your old perception of time being outside your control, consciously correct your language using the updated point of view that time really is what you think it is.

Task Three: Declare your independence from the clock by claiming ownership of your time.

- Look ahead in your calendar to identify a space of time that isn't scheduled, one which you can claim as your own.

- Block out your chosen space of time as an appointment with yourself.

- Make any arrangements you need to secure this time as your own.

- When you go "off the clock," set an alarm to give you a warning of when your time is up. Then, resist the urge to check the time.

- During your time off the clock, allow yourself to be immersed in doing something you love or simply being free.

- As soon as you've enjoyed one session of being off the clock, schedule another.

Task Four: Enhance your freedom by honoring stillness.

- Notice spaces in your day when stillness is available to you.

- When you have an opportunity for stillness, savor just being still. If the urge to give in to distraction arises, take your attention to your breath, so you can return to stillness.

- Practice fasting from distractions. Declare short fasts from texting, social media, or games.

- Use stillness as a doorway to rest and play.

As we approach the end of this chapter, and prepare to move into the final apprenticeship in the alchemy of time, please know that you're not leaving this apprenticeship to ease behind. These four tasks will continue to sustain you in your journey as a Sexy + Soul-full woman. Indeed, these practices occupy such a central role that you can work with them for the rest of your life and never run out of nuances to explore. However, you do have one more myth to discard so that you can fully master the alchemy of time.

Your last apprenticeship will be in rejecting the myth that time is precious.

chapter seven

All Time Is Precious:
An Apprenticeship to Equanimity

THE THIRD AND final myth to undergo transformation is "My time is precious." This pernicious, widely-held fallacy will be subtly reformed into a much more valuable reality: All time is precious.

How is viewing *all* time as precious different from "my time is precious?"

By removing the personal pronoun "my," you uncover the potential for the precious in *every* moment. There is never a time or place or context where the sacred qualities of time go missing. A Sexy + Soul-full way of being is, therefore, abundantly and constantly available.

To gain this new perspective on time, you will enter into your third and final apprenticeship in the alchemy of time, an apprenticeship to equanimity.

What Does it Mean to Be Apprenticed to Equanimity?

Equanimity is a state of being balanced and centered, yet responsive. One friend, herself a very Sexy + Soul-full woman, describes it this way, "When you have equanimity, you're being non-reactive. You develop the ability to see the space between an event occurring and what happens next. And in that space, you can choose how you want to respond. I think of equanimity as inner freedom." In other words, rather than being carried along by events or hijacked by your own reactions, you are able to choose how you want to be.

Often thought of as an even state of mind, equanimity helps us remain calm regardless of the events unfolding. The much revered Zen Buddhist teacher Uchiyama-roshi went so far as to say that experience is just "passing scenery." This view might make it seem that someone with equanimity is completely detached and entirely devoid of emotional responses but that doesn't have to be the case. "While some may think of equanimity as dry neutrality or cool aloofness, mature equanimity produces a radiance and warmth of being," says meditation teacher Gil Fronsdal. "The Buddha described a mind filled with equanimity as 'abundant, exalted, immeasurable, without hostility and without ill-will.'"

I think of equanimity as an essential ingredient of resilience. When I have great equanimity, I am able to "roll with the punches," so to speak. My feelings and reactions still occur, but I am better able to cope with them. Rather than becoming impatient or angry, I can remain in the moment rather than being carried off by my emotions. For example, equanimity saved me from mouthing off to a total stranger not long ago.

My husband and I were visiting a lovely inn, tucked away in a nearby mountain range, with a roaring creek right outside our cottage's door. The inn offers sumptuous dinners every evening but with a catch: The meals are served "family style." Being an introvert, I don't really relish having to make dinnertime small talk with total strangers, but I took a deep breath and sat down across from a man and his son. I quickly realized that the man had a habit of saying "yes, but," which was his way of disagreeing with anything that was brought up in conversation.

After his tenth or eleventh "yes, but," I could feel my temper starting to rise. Immediately, my practice of equanimity paid off. I thought to myself, "I'm starting to feel angry." I took a deep breath, leaned over to my husband, and said, "I'll be back in a little while." He grinned at me, knowing exactly what I really meant, which was more along the lines of, "If I don't leave the table, I'm going to say something I'll regret." Outside, I turned my attention to my surroundings: the flowers in the garden, the sound of rushing water, the coolness of the evening air.

With my emotions calmed, I timed my return to the table to coincide with the food. I hoped that having his mouth full would stop our dining companion from engaging in further conversation. (And it did.) In the past, I would have let a jerk like our disagreeable dinner companion ruin my entire evening but with equanimity, I was able to access my understanding that all time is precious, even the time spent in the company of someone I wouldn't normally choose to sit with.

> *Because all now-moments are equally precious, we can treat our time with reverence.*

Equanimity is a particularly valuable quality to have when moving from "My time is precious," to "All time is precious." When thinking of time as a personal possession, we become eager to hoard, to defend, and to grasp. We can begin to overvalue our time so much that we undervalue the time of others. Worse, by getting deeply attached to our own precious time, we can start to feel resentful of anything or anyone that intrudes and threatens to take some of our precious time away or that seems to interfere with our expectations of what an experience ought to be like for us. Waiting in line, a slow car in the fast lane, being stuck on hold, all grate on our nerves and invite irritation and impatience. Interruptions and crises become our enemies instead of holding possibilities for unexpected opportunities.

Equanimity, on the other hand, argues that time, like experience, is "passing scenery." This realization does not strip time of its worth, however. Each now-moment is equally fleeting and ephemeral, to be experienced fully and then to be released so as to welcome the next now-moment.

Because all now-moments are equally precious, we can treat our time with reverence. With equanimity, it's possible to engage life with a more even, yet still lively, presence. Urgency or wastefulness, impatience or boredom can be set aside. Instead, we become available to the potential of delight inherent in every moment.

WHAT WILL YOU PRACTICE IN YOUR APPRENTICESHIP TO EQUANIMITY?

To begin experiencing the centering effects of your apprenticeship to equanimity, you'll undertake three simple tasks.

- To release your grip on the "my" of "My time is precious," you'll give some time away.

- To gain a more relaxed attitude toward interruptions and crises, you'll practice letting go of your own priorities.

- To embrace the sacred available in ordinary moments, you'll practice welcoming the unexpected with gratitude.

TASK ONE: GIVE TIME AWAY

In many ways, letting go of the myth "My time is precious" is the most difficult of the three. Scarcity, our old friend, always encourages us to hang on to what we have. The lie that scarcity tells is that if you give up possession of what you've got, you'll go wanting, you'll run dry, or you'll come up short. The truth, however, is that grasping time as a possession creates more problems than it solves—like impatience, irritation, stinginess—just to a name a few. Therefore, the first task in your apprenticeship to equanimity is to give some time away. This act of generosity is an important first step in embracing the truth of "All time is precious."

I learned about the importance of generosity courtesy of a research study conducted by Cassie Mogilner, in which Mogilner and her colleagues examined the effects of giving time away to other people. For the experiment, the participants were broken into three groups: one took some small action benefitting someone else, the second took a little extra time for themselves, and the third spent a few minutes on something that was clearly a waste of time (the research subjects circled the letter "e" every time it occurred in a Latin text, but you can substitute noodling on Facebook, tweeting on Twitter, or obsessing over Downton Abbey). Those who did something for someone else even for as few as ten minutes, whether the act was picking up litter in a park or cooking a nice meal for a loved one, reported feeling better about themselves. These "time givers" reported an improved sense of self-efficacy—they had more confidence about their ability to carry out their own aspirations. The "time wasters" or the "time on their self-ers" didn't reap this good feeling about themselves or their ability to get things done: They felt just as ineffective in their use of time as they had before the study started.

"Having done this research, I check myself," says Moligner. "I don't think I was nearly as generous with my time before as I am now. Where now when requests come up for help from colleagues [or] friends, despite the fact that I feel completely stressed [and] time constrained, and I don't feel that I have those spare ten minutes, I remind myself that in fact I do. And if I do take those ten minutes to help out a colleague or friend, that I'll feel like I have more time."

By seeking small opportunities to share time, you grant yourself the opportunity to open your heart with each donation.

What Moligner's research teaches is that holding on to time as personal property doesn't improve your effectiveness; rather, being possessive of time reinforces the feeling of time scarcity. Having done the work of the first apprenticeship in enough, you already have the advantage of knowing how to reduce feelings of time pressure. By practicing the task of giving time away, you'll gain not only a more spacious experience of time but you'll also take a decisive step toward growing in equanimity.

To begin your apprenticeship in giving time away, cultivate your awareness of how you share time with others. It's likely that you're already donating some time each day. The key to this task in the apprenticeship is to be mindful of each act of generosity. In addition, by seeking small opportunities to share time, you grant yourself the opportunity to open your heart with each donation.

{IN UNDERTAKING this practice of giving time away, you're not required to say " yes," to every request. Instead, when a request for time comes to your attention, use the moment to observe your inner landscape. Do you find yourself feeling open and gracious or closed and grasping? Do you recoil from the idea of giving or gravitate toward the act of generosity? Remember, part of equanimity is being conscious of responding rather than reacting. By observing your reactions, you can gain a sense of objectivity over thoughts and feelings, thereby allowing you to seek more possibilities in how you might respond.}

"In an act of giving we're aligning ourselves with certain values. We develop love, compassion, sympathetic joy, and equanimity," writes meditation teacher and author, Sharon Salzberg. "The movement of the heart in practicing generosity mirrors the movement of the heart that lets go inside. If we cultivate a generous heart, then more and more we can unconditionally allow things to be the way they are." Allowing things to be the way they are is the very soul of equanimity.

My own experience of observing my reactions to requests for time tells me that when I'm stressed, my knee-jerk reaction is to feel resentful. However, when I step back from my resentment and ask myself to open my heart, I can see that my initial reaction is based in the lie of scarcity. When I hear myself think, "I don't have time for that now" (with *that* being whatever has been asked of me), I know I am falling prey to this third myth (and the first myth of "more time later," is probably rearing its ugly head again, too). When I center myself, remind myself that I have enough time now, and open my heart, I can view the request with greater equanimity. My more balanced perspective may not result in a 'yes,' but I will be more objective in how I come to my answer. Generosity becomes an option.

At this point, you may be thinking back to the third task in your recent apprenticeship to ease, when I urged you to claim space for yourself in your schedule. By discarding the myth of "My time is precious," you are not being asked to relinquish owning your schedule. Your schedule still belongs to you, even when you give time away. What you are letting go of is the notion that time is too valuable to share or more precious than someone else's time might be. Acts of generosity have a way of creating a greater sense of abundance than holding close to your possessions or time does. The best way to experience this feeling of plenty is to experience it through giving.

You can always find ways to donate a bit of time. When the opportunity arises, do some small act of kindness and cultivate your awareness of giving time away without thought of return. Selfless generosity, when practiced over and over, naturally creates the spacious attitude of equanimity that leads to a full realization of the truth that all time is precious, too precious to keep to yourself.

Once you've begun practicing giving time away, you will grow in your sense of generosity. Your growth will be needed in your second task, when you'll be asked to do something even more revolutionary: Let go of your priorities.

Task Two: Let Go of Your Priorities

In this second task of your apprenticeship to equanimity, you'll practice letting go of your priorities.

Obviously, being able to set priorities is an incredibly useful and important skill in being productive. But in the process of discarding the myth of "My time is precious," constantly clinging to your priorities can be a real hindrance. After all, they're your priorities and losing the personal pronoun is part of the path to embracing "All time is precious."

With equanimity on your side, you are prepared to treasure each moment as precious, instead of valuing only the moments that conform to your priorities.

One of the instances when your priorities can get in the way is when you are interrupted or surprised by the unexpected. Think about the last time you had your priorities firmly in mind and you got hit with an unplanned disruption of your plans. How did you react? If you're anything like me, you might have felt a big surge of irritation.

As a daughter of an elderly mom, my priorities are often interrupted by my mom's needs. I love being able to be available for her when she needs me, but there are days when I wish I could be a hermit and just do my work! Often, however, I find myself rearranging my schedule to accommodate small urgencies and unexpected crises. If I cling to my priorities in the face of these, I find myself feeling grumpy and huffy. By gaining fluency in letting go of my priorities, I've found an avenue for letting go of my irritation and grouchiness, and many times I'm able to be cheerful instead, as I tackle small crises and urgent requests.

Of course, the needs of our families, pets, and coworkers aren't the only ways our priorities get short-circuited. Traffic jams, accidents, broken copiers, computers gone haywire, long waits on hold, delayed flights, and a whole host of other annoyances contribute to the sense that everyone and everything is out to get in the way of our plans. In all these cases, being able to gracefully surrender our priorities and be fully in the moment allows us to experience a sense of inner calm as well as develop a mastery of equanimity.

"When you insist on having only particular kinds of experiences, nothing can deeply touch you. You're too busy judging," wrote Zen teacher, the late Darlene Cohen. To gain equanimity, Cohen, who died of cancer in 2011, practiced making a conscious effort to not always choose what she, herself, preferred. She learned this lesson when her son was small, when she found it oh-so-hard to let go of her own priorities in order to accommodate his. She refused to go to kid's movies or color Easter eggs or take him to Disneyland. These many adventures were wasted on her because, Cohen said, she refused to relinquish her own preferences.

To break her pattern, Cohen began choosing without referencing her preferences. Starting with ice cream flavors, she simply closed her eyes and pointed. This led to letting go of all sorts of other small choices that didn't matter much in the long run, but that gave her practice in releasing her own priorities. Years later, when she was diagnosed with cancer, her practice paid off. "...if you always go with your preference in every matter, then it's harder [to let go] when it does matter—like preferring health to cancer," Cohen wrote.

When you've practiced letting go of your preferences, even in very small ways, you are far more flexible when the more significant events demand this kind of flexibility. With equanimity on your side, you are prepared to treasure each moment as precious, instead of valuing only the moments that conform to your priorities.

If we're willing to let go of our usual way of seeing things, our intuition has a much greater chance of providing its own wisdom and guidance.

To practice letting go of your priorities, I suggest you start small. I began with my underwear drawer. Normally, I prefer to play favorites. I have a favorite bra and a preferred style of panty and a most beloved sort of socks. When I'm consciously practicing letting go of my own priorities, I simply reach in the drawer without looking too closely and whatever I pull out, I wear. Like Darlene Cohen, when I go to the ice cream shop, I choose a flavor at random and make tasting the chilly dessert into an epicurean adventure. If we're going out to eat, I let others choose the restaurant and make an effort to enjoy wherever we go. This practice has provided many benefits including a more relaxed attitude when events are truly outside my control, like flight cancellations and traffic snafus. I am far more able to shrug those off and enjoy wherever I am.

{WHEN YOU decide that you're willing to let go of a small preference, observe your reaction to what you do get. If you feel surprise, disappointment, or irritation, question that feeling. What were you expecting? The next time you let go of another preference, make a conscious decision to release the expectation along with the priority you've assigned to this matter. Each time you make this tiny act of letting go, you'll find it easier to do so again. At the same time, you can cultivate a sense of anticipation. Instead of dreading the unexpected, you might begin to look forward to it instead.}

This practice of letting go of your priorities by way of releasing your preferences is not just a handy way of becoming more patient in the face of delays and obstacles. Letting go of your priorities is an important spiritual practice, too. If you are seeking divine guidance, and you receive it, you're likely to encounter the challenge of letting go of your priorities or having your own way. Embrace this letting go as a form of willingness, a "relaxed decision to 'let pass and let be.'" Relentlessly clinging to your own priorities, on the other hand, can lead to willfulness: a stubborn pursuit of having your own way. Cultivating willingness becomes a path to spiritual refreshment, says psychologist and spiritual teacher, David Benner. "A spirit of willingness invites me to pause and turn to God... letting God bring perspective and clarity [to my actions]. The act of willing surrender is a choice of openness, a choice of abandonment of self determination, a choice of cooperation with God."

This willingness has a way of opening our mind and spirit to creativity as well. If we're willing to let go of our usual way of seeing things, our intuition has a much greater chance of providing its own wisdom and guidance. In the face of willfulness and a tight-fisted hold on our own priorities, however, there is no space for intuition to inhabit.

As an artist, I am constantly challenged to let go of how I think my work ought to turn out and release my desire to make the "right" artistic choices. Instead of fearing that I'll make a mistake, I practice letting my intuition make choices of colors or designs, going with what "feels right," even when my selection doesn't seem to have any logic or reason behind it. Often, I find that the works I create have deeper meaning for me or for their recipients, far beyond what I could have imagined when I was making the piece. My intuition knows things I don't, and only by letting go of my own priorities and plans am I able to let this inner guidance do its job.

Ultimately, letting go of your own priorities is an act of faith and trust. When you cling to always having your own way, you are practicing a form of unhealthy self-reliance that narrows your choices and hems in possibilities. The late Darlene Cohen put it this way, "A life of preference becomes not only self-indulgent but also deadened."

By releasing your priorities from time to time, you learn to open yourself and your options. A few years ago, my husband and I visited one of his colleagues in South Korea. Neither of us speak Korean, and our host had made all sorts of plans for us, many of which included being ferried from place to place by non-English speaking drivers. Our mantra throughout the trip was "Be a leaf in a stream," which meant: Surrender to whatever is happening. I can't recall thinking a judgmental or critical or impatient thought during the entire two-week trip.

{NOT ONLY will your practice of letting go of priorities aid you when unexpected interruptions and crises occur, it can teach you to be more spontaneous in your choice of what to do next. There are times when there are so many tasks hammering at you that it's hard to prioritize among them. In that case, you might simply choose one, rather than worrying about which of the many important and urgent actions to take on first. This simple variation on letting go of your priorities enables you to move forward with some measure of equanimity, even when conditions are stressful and demanding.}

As you grow in your ability to release your own preferences and priorities, you will gain more and more freedom to embrace all time as precious. But your journey in your apprenticeship to equanimity isn't quite finished. You have one more task to master: Welcoming every event with gratitude.

TASK THREE: WELCOME EVERY EVENT WITH GRATITUDE

In the second task ("Let Go of Your Priorities") of your apprenticeship to equanimity, you learned to let go of your priorities in the face of the unexpected. In this third task, you'll extend what you've learned by adding the element of gratitude. Because interruptions are ubiquitous, and often unwelcome intrusions, you'll practice saying "thank you" when you're interrupted. I realize that asking you to practice gratitude in the face of something that is usually unwanted and undesirable is a very counterintuitive request, but hear me out.

The power of gratitude is found when you welcome everything—not just what you've expected, what you wanted, or what you wished for, but everything—with the same warmth of appreciation. The natural partner of gratitude is generosity. A generous heart is one that naturally shares whatever it has. A grateful heart, likewise, is quick to offer thanks no matter what the circumstances or how events are turning out. Gratitude, as a way of being, acknowledges that there are gifts inherent in each passing moment, even when those gifts might not be readily visible or immediately experienced. Thus, being able to welcome each moment with gratitude, no matter what the moment holds, is an important step toward embracing all time as precious.

Like love, joy, and hope, gratitude is a powerful, positive emotion and, in my view, is the only positive emotion that we can learn to summon "on demand," so to speak. It's hard to muster love or awe or hope at a moment's notice, but gratitude is different. You can bring gratitude into being simply by thinking of what you are grateful for or by offering thanks. So while you may not feel grateful when an interruption comes along, you can speak gratitude into being by saying (aloud or silently), a heartfelt and genuine "thank you."

We all know the feelings of annoyance, frustration, loss of concentration, and impatience that arise when an interruption comes along. These are all negatives that make some of us truly loathe being interrupted. Part of the reason why we get so testy is because our human brains tend to discount the value of delayed rewards in favor of immediate gratification. However, gratitude has the power to mitigate impatience and other negative emotions.

A generous heart is one that naturally shares whatever it has.

In experiments aimed at understanding the effects of gratitude on financial decisions, David DeSteno and his colleagues learned that when participants were asked to practice gratitude, they were more patient. Instead of selecting immediate, smaller value rewards, the grateful participants were more willing to wait for later rewards of higher value. Other participants, who were not primed with gratitude, were more impatient and usually opted for short-term gains.

In another study, DeSteno and his team found that gratitude changes people's attitudes towards rendering help. When participants were given the opportunity to feel gratitude toward one person, the grateful folks were far more likely to offer heart-felt assistance to another person. This, DeSteno says, could be a driver of important and much needed social change because gratitude felt by one person is played forward in helping a third party. "So next time you have the opportunity to say 'thank you,' don't let it ring hollow," writes DeSteno, "Embrace the gratitude; feel it as deeply as you can, because in so doing, you're actually increasing the odds that in the future we'll all have more for which to be grateful."

To give yourself an experience of heart-felt gratitude in this moment, take a deep breath and place your right hand over your heart. Call to mind someone you love and tell that person "Thank you." Breathe in your gratitude for their love and breathe out your thanks. Simply dwell in this experience of gratitude for several seconds. Before the moment of gratitude passes, prime yourself to recall this moment the next time you say the words "thank you." You might say to yourself, "The next time I say 'thank you,' I will remember this experience of gratitude." Afterward, when an interruption occurs, take a deep breath and say "thank you," either aloud or to yourself with as much sincerity as you can muster.

On the day I was writing this section, I received an email encouraging me to take part in a voluntary earthquake drill. "Today at, 10:16 AM, conduct a voluntary earthquake drill in your work area. Drop, seek cover, and hold on to the cover for 60 seconds, then resume your daily activities." At 10:17 AM, when my dog and I crawled out from under my desk, I said, "Thank you!" It was a genuine thanks as much to the interruption of the drill as for the fact it was only a drill and not a real earthquake.

You may never come to truly welcome interruptions, but what you will find is a greater ease in releasing your irritation as you practice offering thanks instead. Simultaneously, you will grow in your ability to embrace the truth of all time as precious, when you experience heart-felt gratitude for each and every moment, regardless of the circumstances.

SUMMARY

In your apprenticeship to equanimity, you've practiced three tasks intended to move you from "My time is precious," to "All time is precious." Each task is summarized as follows.

Task One: Give time away.

- Cultivate your awareness of how you share time with others and be mindful of each act of generosity.

- When someone asks for time, observe your inner landscape. As you become more skillful in noting your own reactions, you gain greater objectivity and grow in equanimity. Your more balanced perspective opens the door to generosity as a possibility.

- Look for small opportunities to donate a bit of time. When the opportunity arises, do some small act of kindness and cultivate your awareness of giving time away without thought of return.

Task Two: Let go of your priorities.

- Start practicing letting go of your preferences in small ways. Choose an item off the menu by pointing without looking or invite someone else to choose for you. Grab an item of clothing to wear without trying to decide what you'd most like to wear that day.

- When unexpected events or last minute requests occur, practice putting aside your own priorities. Make a note of your reaction to releasing what you had planned. Next time, see if you can let go of your reaction along with your priority.

- When urgent priorities are competing, simply choose one without debating which action is the "best." Using the lessons you learned in your apprenticeship to enough time now, pick something and get down to work right away.

Task Three: Welcome every event with gratitude.

- Practice the experience of heart-felt gratitude accompanied by saying "Thank you." Take a deep breath and put your hand on your heart, then think of someone you love. Breathe in gratitude and breathe out a meaningful "Thank you." Before the moment passes, set the intention to remember this gratitude experience the next time you speak the words, "Thank you."

- When interruptions occur, say "Thank you," either aloud or silently to yourself. Observe how your heart responds to the interruptions when you greet with them gratitude.

PART III

PUTTING LOVE INTO ACTION

I once asked a bird,

"How is it that you fly in this gravity of darkness?"

She responded,

"Love lifts Me."

—HAFIZ

In the first part of this book, we explored the past and (re)discovered what we love. Then, we examined the three destructive myths about time and, by discarding those, learned how to practice the alchemy of time—to make time for what we love. In this third, and final, part of the book, we'll talk about how to put our love(s) into action.

Productivity, in the more traditional sense, is about adding action to plans and goals to get things done. The Sexy + Soul-full approach adds love to this equation. Direction is best discerned by a heart that's centered on your loves. Plans are made which direct actions that are carried out from a place of love, infusing your every step with grace.

One of the keys to putting love into action is an understanding that love is both a verb and a noun. As a verb, love is something you do— love is an active way of being that expresses your caring, communicates your passion, and moves you toward your most heart-felt desires. On the other hand, love is a noun: You have loves. Hopefully, you discovered some of the nouns that are synonymous with your loves in the first section of the book.

Understanding this dual nature of love as both a verb and noun is helpful because love is both something you have and an action you carry out. When experienced as only one or the other, love is deprived of much of its effectiveness. However, when you combine the having with the doing, love is amplified and empowered. For example, if you have a love of nature and you express that love through creating a wildlife-friendly garden, then your love grows—literally and figuratively.

The ability to both have love and do love simultaneously becomes a good litmus test for creating a vision for your life and work, and for determining what direction you might want to go in. You can have a very profound love for something but then find yourself struggling to express your love in actions. This difficulty might be a signal that you're heading in the wrong direction. Often, I encounter this roadblock when I love the idea of a particular project or an imagined direction but loathe the work that's required of me. If I cannot summon love as the motive and driver of my actions, that's usually an indication that I'm on the wrong road. I love the idea of being a yoga teacher, for instance, but when I delve into the necessary studies, love is nowhere to be found. I loved the notion of becoming a spiritual director but couldn't stomach the second year of training.

In the next chapter, I'll share how my love-hate relationship with goals has led me to emphasize effort and intention instead. I'll guide you through a process of creating a compelling and love-oriented compass heading for your future. You'll have the opportunity to reflect on your recent past, construct a "common-sense" timeline for the years ahead, and then discern a direction for your efforts based on what's calling to your soul.

A vision without action is merely a pleasant dream. You'll need a heart-felt plan to move your aspirations from the abstract and ephemeral to the concrete and realized. The chapter entitled, "Taking Vision Into Action" will provide you with the steps to take to complete a full draft of your plan for the future.

I've come to appreciate the power of making and keeping promises to myself as a means of putting love to work. Before you dive into doing,

I invite you to explore what being reliable to and for yourself means. If, in the past, you've struggled with realizing your most closely-held aspirations, becoming more reliable is key to your future progress. In "Keeping Your Promises to Yourself," you'll learn about the joy of completion, the power of setting and keeping intentions, and how to connect your aspirations with accountability.

All actions produce reactions. Sometimes, your efforts will produce favorable and delightful results. At other times, your exertions will yield responses that you'd rather they didn't. Either way, receiving your results with grace will help you to weather adversity with aplomb and allow you to enjoy success with equal poise. "Receiving Results With Grace" is about how to receive results with gratitude and celebration. In this chapter, I also address the possibility of outright failure and when to consider that quitting is the right response to negative results.

Productivity, in the more traditional sense, is about adding action to plans and goals to get things done.

chapter eight

Setting Direction with Discernment

I HAVE A bit of a love-hate relationship with goals.

On the one hand, I know that having goals can be helpful. Goals, by setting an end-point of sorts, give us a way to know whether or not we've reached our intended destination. Without a goal, you could end up wandering around and around, never getting anywhere. But with a clear goal in mind, you know what direction to take, how far you have to travel, and where you want to go. That suggests that you need to set goals in order to successfully put your love(s) into action.

My experiences, however, have left me feeling less than enthusiastic about extolling the virtues of goal setting. In the past, I've gone through phases of setting lofty goals only to fall short again and again. My failures left me feeling that creating goals is a mixed bag. Yes, goals tell me where to go and define my destination but an out-of-reach, unmet goal can become a painful reminder of what I wanted to achieve and didn't accomplish.

Here's an example of what I mean. In 2010, I decided to walk a three-day event intended to raise money for the fight against breast cancer. I had two goals: to walk the entire, 60-mile course and to meet the fundraising minimum of $3,000. I trained diligently, putting in dozens of miles to ready my body for the effort ahead. A fan of my podcast learned what I was up to, and unbeknownst to me, put out a call for donations. Suddenly, gifts poured in, and I exceeded my fundraising goal by a large margin. Feeling incredibly optimistic, I arrived in Seattle on a bright September morning to begin my walk. I completed

By envisioning your future and using that vision as a compass heading, you get the advantages of setting goals without getting boxed in by the typical either-or, success-failure dead end.

the first 20 miles easily but on the second day, I didn't take proper care of myself. On the third morning, I could barely move but I managed to hobble the last couple of miles (after catching a ride and skipping most of that day's course). From a goals standpoint, I had one success (the fundraising) and one failure (the walk). In the final analysis, however, I came away feeling disappointed and ashamed of my performance.

The following year, I wanted a do-over. Fiscally, I didn't get enough donations and wrote a sizable check out of my own pocket to meet the minimum donation requirement. Physically, I easily walked all 60 miles without a single blister. Even though my results were mixed, just as they were the year before, my perception of the second event was entirely different. Instead of looking at the event through a goals-tinted lens, I had set an intention to be fully present and savor the entire experience—no matter how it turned out.

So how was having an intention different from setting goals? Often, the success of a results-based goal is beyond my control: I can do all the right things and still not obtain my desired outcome. For example, in 2010, I did my best to train properly and not only did I fail to complete the course, but I also lost four toenails! Fulfilling my intention during my do-over, however, was entirely up to me. I knew that I could choose to be fully present and savor each moment of the experience. Being in control of the actions needed to satisfy my intention transformed my mixed results into an entirely fulfilling and memorable adventure.

This is but one example, but most of my experiences with goal setting are similarly equivocal. The problem with pursing a specific goal is that the result is so either-or: Either I achieved my goal or I didn't. There's no room in this binary sort of failure-success scenario for the heady blend of achievements, mistakes, successes, lessons, disappointments, failures, and downright luck of which most endeavors are comprised.

If your experiences have been similar to mine, you, too, might be feeling a little wary of goal setting. And yet, I believe that we need some way to set a direction for our actions. After all, we need a compass heading so that we can take effective actions that allow us to contribute our gifts to the world around us. The question is: What is the best way to set direction?

I've come to believe that creating an intentions-based vision of the future is a sound alternative to goal setting. A vision is a picture of what you want to do or who you want to be in some future age or during a coming season of your life. This picture may be richly textured but is best when painted with very broad strokes. Rather than focusing on exact details of how your future will unfold, a vision is composed of patterns, colors, and gestures—indications which give a compelling idea of what might be in store for you without painting you into a corner of pursuing a particular outcome.

By envisioning your future and using that vision as a compass heading, you get the advantages of setting goals without getting boxed in by the typical either-or, success-failure dead end. Using intentions and focusing on your efforts allows you to engage with what you can control (your actions) while gaining some detachment from what you can't control (your results).

For an unhurried experience of completing the tasks in this chapter, I suggest you claim at least half a day for yourself. Having an entire day or even a weekend would be even better. If your life won't accommodate that much uninterrupted you-time, block out several small spaces (an hour a piece is plenty) over the course of a week or two to allow yourself plenty of room to complete all the aspects of each task, including rest and contemplation. The aim isn't to rush to a vision; instead, I want to give you enough space to create a useful "first draft" that you'll revise later.

All too often, we're in a hurry to crystalize a vision and then get to work! The urgency is understandable: You want to start realizing the joys of what you've envisioned right away. But rushing through the visioning process is a mistake. Living your life purposefully, according to an envisioned future, is a big undertaking. You're making a huge investment in yourself when you put your loves on the line and center your actions on your most heart-felt aspirations. I encourage you to be intentional and slow down to really savor the experience of creating a meaningful vision of your potential future.

There are many tools available to help you to create a vision. In the pages that follow, I'll present one of the approaches that I've found most helpful. Before you begin the first task, sit quietly and cultivate an awareness of your breath. If you wish, say a prayer for guidance, clarity, and wisdom as you undertake this process. Lighting a candle, burning incense, smudging with sage, or some other small ritual may help you to settle yourself and to provide a sense of the sacred as you prepare yourself for this important work. If you're spacing the process out over more than one day, take care to open each session by settling and centering yourself through meditation, stillness, or prayer.

REFLECTING ON YOUR PAST

To begin creating your vision for the future, I suggest you take a look back at your past. By first engaging in a process of review and reflection, you will glean insights and learning to inform your thinking about what you might want to undertake for the future.

Before you begin, gather your appointment calendars, journals, and any other materials you need to assist you in recalling major events and significant experiences. Other supplies you might enjoy include big sheets of butcher paper, a sketch book, or materials that will allow you to construct a timeline or a list that helps you to see where you've been and what's been happening. You might enjoy using colored markers and sticky notes, too.

The timeframe you select for your review is up to you. Simply use whatever length of time you feel will give you the most complete picture of how life has been for you recently. The intention for the exercise is to examine the "recent" past, but you get to decide when "recent" begins. For example, my dad passed away nearly four years ago and that event was incredibly significant for me—so I would choose to begin my review around the time of his passing.

Starting at the point of your choosing, review your calendar and supporting materials to create a timeline of the past. You don't need to make an exhaustive list of every little moment—the goal is simply to map out, in broad strokes, the events or experiences that affected you most deeply over the span of time you've selected. When I do this process during my annual birthday retreat, I scrawl out a narrative in my journal and then identify the larger, more significant events that I want to put on my year's timeline. I employ a sort-of shorthand to make the process manageable like "started coaching with [client's name]," or "attended mosaic conference." I attempt to keep my narrative in chronological order but if a memory pops up, I capture it immediately. While this kind of review can become very time consuming, I suggest that you budget about thirty minutes to an hour per year's time and discipline yourself to keep moving along.

When you've completed your review, re-read your narrative and allow yourself to recall any additional events or memories. By lingering over this process, you'll have a much better chance of relaxing and letting your mind offer up any jewels that might be buried more deeply in your memory. I often find that significant insights or turning points in my review were missed and those seem to pop in my consciousness only after I've given myself time to "review my review." If you feel stuck, or nothing is coming to mind, simply sit and attend to your breath for at least three to five minutes. Once you feel satisfied that you've captured all that's available to you, take a big sheet of paper and construct a timeline of the "big ticket" events and memories. These might be birthdays or times of loss, trips, promotions, graduations, or any other events that stand out as especially meaningful to you.

Now, take a look back at your loves that you (re)discovered while reading the first section of the book. Review the timeline you just created and see if you can map your loves onto the experiences and events you identified. For example, in my three-year review, I noted when I discovered mosaic, a significant recent development in my love of art and beauty. When you're finished adding your loves to your timeline, consider offering prayers of gratitude or words of thanks for what's gone before—the gifts, the struggles, the celebrations, the mournings, and any other aspects of your past that you've identified. Also, check in with yourself: How is your energy? Be gentle with yourself, especially if you've recalled very painful or otherwise difficult happenings. Take a break for rest or a walk if needed.

Next, get your journal or a fresh sheet of paper and, using your timeline, glean some insights. Here are some journaling prompts to stimulate your reflection:

The most important lessons I've learned are...

When I look for what's going well, I see...

What have my most informative failures taught me?

My biggest insights are...

When I am at my very best, I notice...

My greatest strengths are...

What are my gifts? When I use my gifts to the best of my ability, what do I contribute?

Take your time in answering these questions—don't rush. If you get stuck on one question, simply leave it behind and move on to another. Afterward, you might want to create bullet lists or other ways of highlighting certain points that stand out to you. In addition to contemplating these journaling prompts, you might benefit from a structured exploration of your strengths using an online inventory.

This is another good moment for a check-in. Do you need a rest or a break? Do whatever you need to do in order to stay fresh for this process before moving on to constructing a timeline for the future.

Constructing a Timeline for the Future

In the first step of setting direction, you reviewed your past to draw insight from your experience and to identify your gifts and strengths. Next, you'll construct a timeline of the future. You'll use this timeline as a framework for sketching out the first draft of your vision.

Decide how far ahead you'd like to reach: one, three, five, ten years, or some other time period that seems right. Envisioning a very long span of time (like, for example, twenty-five years) might be very challenging but if that's what calls to you, go for it!

To create your timeline, you'll need a long sheet of paper or, if you prefer, several sheets that represent the number of years your plan will cover. On one end of your timeline, note your current age and the current year. On the other end of your timeline sheet(s), make a mark of some sort and note the year and how old you'll be at the end of your chosen span. If there are significant people in your life, mark their ages at both ends of the timeline, too—your husband, parents, children, even your pets. When I did this exercise recently, I realized that my "puppy" would be seventeen years old, if we're lucky enough to have him that long. Make marks and note the years that coincide, more or less, with the halfway point and midpoints between the ends. Again, note future ages for yourself and your important others at these other points along your timeline. When you've concluded this section, you'll have a timeline divided into four parts of roughly equal length.

Take this opportunity to ask yourself what changes you expect in your and other people's lives during this future period. Your children might graduate from college, for example—note when you imagine that event might occur. If your husband is contemplating retirement and that falls in your time span, mark it down. If you're uncertain, make a list of questions for the important people in your life. My husband brought up that he'll have a sabbatical year—one which might include a big overseas trip—and that kind of event needed to be on my timeline!

What other events might occur in this time span that you can anticipate based on age or stage of life? Make notes for all of those. If you have elderly parents or someone who is struggling with significant illness, your heart may know that this person might depart during this time span. If so, make a *Successful discernment does not imply that you'll experience a set of desired outcomes.* note somewhere as a means of acknowledging this or any other uncertain yet somewhat anticipated event. Making these kinds of notations may already be suggesting what your future might be like and if so, capture those ideas when they appear and park them somewhere safe for now.

(Sticky notes work great for capturing these glimpses of the future and holding them safely in storage for later consideration.)

When your future timeline feels as complete as possible (for now), spend some time gazing at your annotations and allow your imagination to wander just a bit. At the end of my ten year timeline, I'll be sixty-three! Frankly, I needed a little time to let that fact soak in before I moved to the next part of creating a vision for myself. You, too, might need some space to take in what you're seeing ahead of you, so again, be gentle and responsive to your needs.

DISCERNING SOUL-FULL DIRECTION

The third phase of setting direction is discerning a soul-full direction. Discernment is best undertaken when you're willing to know what the deepest desires of your heart are, and you are willing to act on that knowledge. For this reason, I suggest that you undertake discernment carefully. That said, discernment isn't to be feared—you may uncover a surprising inclination but, if done appropriately, you will never be led in a direction that is destructive to you or your loved ones.

One point to consider is that discernment doesn't supply a picture of the future nor a list of results you'll obtain. You will learn only what direction to go in and what to attempt to do. Successful discernment does not imply that you'll experience a set of desired outcomes. Likewise, difficulties and failures are not necessarily indicators that your discernment was mistaken. No matter how you go about choosing a direction, you will always incur risk. The beauty of discernment, beyond its tried-and-true value as an ancient method of decision making, is that it provides a means of making a thoughtful, heart-felt, yet still somewhat objective choice.

The amount of time required to discern direction varies. You may experience a knowing with clarity that is unmistakable and instantaneous, as I did in 1990 when I realized that I wanted to live and work at Rara Avis in Costa Rica. At other times, discernment may go on for days, weeks, or even longer. A young woman in my community recently completed a year-long discernment process about going into religious life. For most of us, however, discerning direction isn't about a life-long commitment or changing the whole direction of our lives but rather one of asking ourselves: "Where do I go from here?"

EXERCISE

Here is a method of discernment in four simple steps.

- Step 1. First, practice stillness. Just as you did in during your apprenticeship to ease, regularly quiet yourself and step out of the stream of life. You might use a walking meditation or a set time for prayer or contemplation. Whatever method or approach you choose, attempt to remain in silence rather than reading, listening to music, or being entertained in some way.

- Step 2. While you are still, listen to your heart. What are your deepest desires? What do you most long to do or to be a part of? As you did earlier in this chapter, consider the times you are at your best. Ask how your gifts and strengths might make a difference in the world. Think about what needs you see that you feel drawn toward addressing. One way to identify your heart's deepest longings is to attend to what repeatedly arises in your consciousness. If no one cause or direction stands out, look for commonalities among whatever comes up. You can always make a sincere request of your heart to speak to you and ask the Divine to come to your assistance in listening to what your heart has to say.

• Step 3. Qualify the options that come to mind. If you are practicing stillness and sincerely inquiring what your heart's deepest desires are, you will begin to see possibilities. Discard any options that are clearly wrong—morally, ethically, or legally—and reject any possibility that is clearly harmful to yourself or someone else. Retain all the other options, for now, even if one or more of them are not immediately attractive to you.

• Step 4. The final step is to decide which option(s) to pursue. There are several ways to work through the remaining possibilities. One of my favorite ways of discerning options is to ask which idea suggests itself to me persistently and consistently. If an idea occurs over and over, that's often a good sign that the possibility deserves serious consideration. You can look for which possibilities are clearly mismatches for your gifts and strike those from the list. List out the remaining options and brainstorm the pros and cons. Often, this kind of analysis will narrow down the possibilities to two or three candidates.

Paradoxically, discernment doesn't include identifying which option might bring you the greatest happiness. Humans are notoriously poor at predicting which choices will bring the greatest long-term satisfaction. Instead, discernment is concerned with which option elicits the greatest sense of peace. Pay very close attention to your emotional responses as you examine the possibilities: Which option moves your heart with love? When you think about embracing one path over the other, which one evokes calm, joy, or a feeling of being at home? One caveat: Refrain from fantasizing about how a particular option might turn out. Instead, keep to the present moment and simply consider the choice before you and the information you have at hand.

Once one option stands out as most appealing—based on a deep sense of love—select that route and end the discernment.

I know it's tempting to waffle back and forth or to try to keep your options open. Don't. The point of discernment is to trust the sense of peace and love you receive and go with that direction. But what if two (or more) options move your heart very strongly and nothing stands out? At that point, if all are equally appealing, you can simply pick either one with the trust that there is no wrong decision because you eliminated the harmful options early on. Remember: you are not choosing your destiny! You are only choosing what direction to go in and what you will attempt to accomplish.

Let's look at a real-life example of what soul-full discernment looks like in action.

In 2006, when Amy and I met, she was considering leaving her social work job. She had discovered that she had a deep desire to provide churches with faith-based sex education but she was worried that she wouldn't be able to make a living as an educator. To help her discern her direction, I asked her a simple question: "What is God moving you toward?"

Amy writes, "I made a sign with that question, 'What is God moving me toward?' in all kinds of fonts and colors, cut it up, and pasted them all over my house and in my car." Every time she felt stuck, she'd ask herself the question again and then would take a small step in the direction she felt she was being led. Fast forward to 2014.

"So here I am making most of my living teaching people about sexuality education in faith communities. In the national setting, and for my denomination. Because that's what God has been leading me toward. It's really the only logical explanation," explains Amy.

From the very beginning of our work together, Amy expressed her passion for what she ultimately ended up doing. Her discernment included whether or not to leave her social work job (she did) and which path to pursue afterward. She considered becoming a parenting coach because that seemed more feasible. However, by consistently and gently stepping toward the direction in which she felt she was being led, she is passionately and joyfully living out her vision for her life.

When you know where you're headed, it's time to undertake the next chapter and take vision into action.

chapter nine

Taking Vision into Action with a Heart-Centered Plan

Now that you have reflected on the past, drawn insights and lessons from your experiences, and discerned a direction for the future, you are prepared to take your vision into action by creating a flexible, yet robust, plan. The plan you'll create will be centered in your loves and will be based on your most heartfelt desires, just as your discernment process was.

To create your plan, you will overlay your desired direction onto the future timeline you initiated in the previous chapter. No matter what direction you've discerned, your journey must start where you are! Your life already has a rhythm and a trajectory; the intention is to honor where you are now while creating your plan for where you want to go in the future. The timeline you've created is meant to represent this trajectory of your current reality. In as much as possible, your trajectory is the "forecast" of the landscape of your life in the years ahead. If you live, you know you'll get older (even if that fact is hard to

Milestones are potential outcomes that convey information about progress toward an envisioned destination.

accept) and your loved ones will age, too. The events and anticipated changes you identified are ways of acknowledging that you have certain, pre-existing realities to take into account as part of your planning.

ANTICIPATE COMMON-SENSE MILESTONES ALONG YOUR FUTURE PATH

Your next step will be to create some new, "candidate" timelines for your discerned direction. The first of these candidate timelines will be a forecast of how you think your path might unfold. If, for example, you've discerned a desire to become a yoga teacher, then your path over a course of five years might "end" in teaching. Between that milestone and now, going in backwards order, you would be deciding in what capacity to teach (e.g., getting hired or starting your own studio), earning your teacher certification, enrolling in a program, completing pre-requisites required by the school you've chosen, and choosing a school. Each of these events are "common-sense milestones" that you have good reason to expect to pass on your way to teaching yoga.

You may need to do a bit of research to be able to forecast the common-sense milestones for your discerned direction. Approaches might include seeking someone who has done what you want to do, contacting professional societies or associations, searching the internet for role models, or the like. A well-trained coach can also be a great help in keeping your process moving forward and helping you to think through choices. Remember, you are not deciding what will happen! You are simply determining a possible path that forecasts some milestones you are likely to encounter as you are making progress in the desired direction.

To clarify a distinction: Milestones are not goals. Milestones are potential outcomes that convey some kind of information about progress, or lack thereof, toward an envisioned destination. Let's say you're traveling along a trail and you see a stone mile marker that reads "Mile 5." If you were expecting to reach Mile 5 because you passed Mile 4 a while back, then all is well and good. But if you passed Mile 11 and you find yourself at Mile 5, that's a different story. You might be lost, you might have missed a turn, or you might have amnesia! In any event, you'd need to check to make sure you're on the right route.

When it comes to planning your way toward an envisioned future, milestones work much in the same way that markers along trails do. When a given milestone is encountered, that marker communicates that you're moving in the direction you envisioned and that your efforts are paying off as you anticipated. Conversely, if you're not reaching your milestones, that might be an indication that you need to rethink your strategy or return to discernment.

Some years ago, a good friend of mine discerned a call to become a minister. She did her homework and learned what the expected milestones along her path would be from where she was to becoming a full-time pastor. Through her research, she also figured out how many years her journey might take—especially if she didn't dawdle along the way. She's now an interim pastor, right on schedule to answer a permanent call by a church when the right opportunity arises.

Draft Candidate Timelines That Will Affect Your Planning

Once you've established a possible timeline for your discerned direction, you'll create another set of timelines based on three to five areas of your life that are most important to your long-term direction. These choices might be drawn from your love(s) or areas of your life, like your physical health, finances, relationships, career, family, spiritual life, or creativity. I encourage you to limit your initial planning process to three to five areas because when you slice categories too finely, the results can become overcomplicated and confusing. You can always return to this process and look at your life from a different set of criteria so for now, seek a simple route that feels sufficient for a "first draft."

Beginning with the first category, ask yourself: How will following my discerned direction affect this area of my life? As an aspiring yoga teacher, you might consider your physical health and ask: What do I expect I'll need to plan for, physically, as I pursue teaching yoga full-time? If you're a young woman, you might be anticipating a pregnancy—so thinking about how yoga will affect your body before, during, and after childbirth would be part of your planning. Financially, your effort toward becoming a yoga teacher will mean incurring expenses along with changes in income as you transition from one career to another—your financial timeline should include these transitions. As before, your aim is to identify a set of common-sense milestones, some of which may already be on your foundational "reality-based" timeline that you created in the previous chapter.

One of the gifts of this kind of planning is flexibility; your plan can be adjusted to events as they occur. You don't have to be on a schedule! Instead, you're asking: Over the next however-many years, what kinds of events and challenges might be on the horizon, and how do I want to approach those within the context of this direction I want my life to take? You can't anticipate everything—no one can—but you can consult your intuition, wisdom, and experience to select which areas of your life would benefit from having a well-thought out plan.

To be honest, this is the kind of thinking about the future we rarely do even though we can draw significant benefits from thinking and planning this way. Sometimes, just by *Very much like a garden, your plan will flourish with careful attention & get choked with weeds if neglected.* thinking through what a trajectory really requires is enough to either deepen our commitment or help us face the fact that we actually are not up to making that kind of effort or investment.

In my own life, I anticipated that our old dog would pass on, and there will be a new puppy in our home someday. I don't know when that adoption will happen but I can anticipate certain events like going to a shelter, finding a spot for the puppy crate, and introducing our remaining dog to his new little brother or sister. Knowing what is required of me physically, financially, and emotionally during the period between puppy and mature dog gives me all kinds of valuable information about timing the acquisition of a new "fur-kid." One of my friends brought a puppy home and *then* realized how stressful puppyhood is. She and her husband weren't up to that kind of effort! Fortunately, they easily found a "forever home" for the dog. However, it would have been more helpful to have had that reality check long before their heartbreaking realization that they'd made a mistake.

That brings us to combining your timelines to create a complete picture of where you might be headed.

COMBINE YOUR TIMELINES TO COMPLETE A DRAFT OF YOUR PLAN

After you've created your forecasts of common-sense milestones for your discerned direction along with three to five important areas of your life, you will return to your foundational, "reality-based" timeline and put together a comprehensive future forecast.

Starting with the present, compare your timelines year-by-year and look for conflicts. By conflicts, I mean events or plans that might be mutually exclusive or interfere with each other. For example, if you're thinking of doing your yoga teacher training in Costa Rica and your daughter is getting married that same month—well, those plans might collide in unfortunate ways. (Although, some mothers of brides might love to be out of the country during the wedding planning!)

By comparing timelines, you can adjust your timing, anticipate conversations and negotiations with people affected by your plans, and identify seasons of your life that will challenge or nurture your progress. As you note these details and insights, capture them using sticky notes so you can tie your thinking to your forecast. You'll later put these items into a tickler file so you can refer to them in a timely way.

I'm thinking of walking the Camino de Santiago de Compostela to celebrate my 60th birthday. The proposed pilgrimage is on my ten-year plan, along with the training and preparation that will be necessary to have a successful and enjoyable walk. There's no reason to begin that work now—the trip is seven years in the future! But I do have all the notes in my tickler file so that when I celebrate my 59th birthday, I can get my rear in gear. Of course, realizing these kinds of long-range plans depends on my ability to reliably make and keep promises to myself, a topic we'll study in the following chapter.

When you've completed your timeline comparisons, you can merge your timelines into a single forecast that includes both your common-sense milestones along with your anticipated realities. Congratulations! You now have a full draft of your plan!

Your forecast is not the last word in how you'll go about moving toward your future, of course. Your plan is a living, breathing, and ever-changing creation—it truly does has a life of its own. Like a tree, it will grow and branch out, and sprout and bear fruit. Likewise, it will have seasons of waiting, flowering, stasis, and dying back. Like any good gardener, tending your plan through watering, pruning, fertilizing, and harvesting is all up to you. And very much like a garden, your plan will flourish with careful attention and get choked with weeds if neglected.

If there's one lesson that gardening has taught me, it's that the seasons do not tolerate procrastination! If I forget to plant seeds in their appropriate month, I get no harvest of yummy vegetables during the summer. You can put your plan aside and ignore your timelines, true. But if you wish to have some chance of harvesting the fruits of your aspirations in the season of life you've forecasted for them, you must take sincere and devoted action in advance. Your sincere and devoted effort is *not* the key to your success; sincere and devoted effort *is* your success!

By focusing on the sincerity and devotion of your actions, you avoid the trap of traditional goal-setting which predicates success on your achievements and accomplishments. For the Sexy + Soul-full woman, as long as you are working in service of the purpose to which you were called, you are being successful.

Use Long-Term Direction to Inform Short-term Actions

To experience this Sexy + Soul-full success, you will use your long-term direction to inform your short-term actions. Using your plan, create a fresh timeline for the next twelve months. As you did before, forecast for the coming year based on current and anticipated realities. Along with these realities, map out the milestones that you've created that are likely to fall within the next twelve months. Between those big milestones, you'll need to identify smaller milestones that mark shorter periods of time.

For example, at the time of this writing, a major milestone is a few months away: the launch of this book. I have identified many smaller milestones that I expect to pass on the way to that larger and much anticipated book launch. These include getting the book cover design finalized, launching my newly-redesigned website, and helping my publicist create my press kit. Your own list of near-term milestones doesn't have to be exhaustive but you do want enough information to clearly understand the actions you need to undertake and roughly what the timing of those actions will be.

Once you have a twelve-month timeline, map out your next 30 days. Sketch out the month ahead with your forecast of what will occur and when. Remember, the intention of this exercise is to identify what the focus of your sincere and devoted effort will be as you move toward the direction you've discerned. Keeping to the example of becoming a yoga teacher, striving for daily asana practice would be part of those efforts over the next thirty days. Depending on the timing of your plan, there will be other actions that must be taken in the next month to improve the chances of passing other, larger milestones in the future.

I know this has been a long journey of planning, and you must be itching to get started on taking action! Before you launch yourself into doing, there is one more plan to create: the plan for your next seven days.

In every journey, there are very small actions that move you forward. As a prospective yoga teacher, your small actions would be those daily practices along with discrete actions that your larger planning efforts suggested to you. The weekly review—an idea I've adapted from David Allen's *Getting Things Done*—is the regular process of planning the next seven days.

{For your weekly review, you'll review your calendar for each event and note whatever advance preparation is required. You also want to note any possible follow up action or to-do. When I do my weekly review, for example, I know that client appointments include reviewing recent past conversations and, afterward, writing a summary or carrying out other kinds of follow ups for the client. All these actions find homes on my task lists, which I consult frequently throughout the week to guide my actions. In this respect, I still follow much of what I learned during my days of practicing *Getting Things Done*.}

After you've completed your weekly review, you have a solid plan in hand to inform your actions over the next seven days. Hurray! You are ready to put your love into action! On your calendar, mark out a recurring appointment with yourself for your weekly review. After thirty days (roughly four weeks), you'll need to revisit the monthly part of your process. Annually, you'll have another review and planning session to complete as you live your way through the forecast you created.

Before we move on to the next chapter, take a moment to pray a blessing for yourself and to celebrate the creation of your plan. This is a big deal! You have discerned direction and created a meaningful plan for a significant portion of your future. Congratulate yourself on this accomplishment. Many women never make this kind of intentional investment in their futures. Imagine how the world would be different if all of us discerned our deepest loves and purposefully pursued those callings! Your contribution to the world is all the more tangible now that you have a plan. In celebration, the next chapter will gift you with a very important skill: Making and keeping the promises you make to yourself will help you bring your plan to fruition.

chapter ten

Keeping Your Promises to Yourself

RELIABILITY, OR THE ability to make and keep promises, is the fulcrum on which all productivity rests. There are two kinds of reliability: external and internal or self-reliability.

External reliability is the one you're most familiar with: the practice of making and keeping commitments to other people. Self-reliability is the practice of being able to trust your own promises—those that you make to yourself and that no one else knows about.

External reliability is at the heart of all relationships. When a person can depend on you to do what you say you'll do, you are reliable, and that creates the soil for trust to take root and grow. When this mutual trust exists, it brings a peace and security to the relationship. For the Sexy + Soul-full woman, this kind of trust has a sacred quality to it. It's rooted and solid, holy and hopeful.

Conversely, when someone isn't reliable, trust is weakened, damaged, or destroyed altogether. Resentment can be sown if you are struggling to do your part and the other party isn't holding up their part of the agreement. Without trust, relationships can't thrive and grow. Without trust, there is always anxiety about whether the people we rely on will help us hold our lives together.

Reliability, or the ability to make and keep promises, is the fulcrum on which all productivity rests.

Self-reliability is the other half of the reliability equation. Unlike external reliability, in which another person is impacted by whether you keep your commitments, self-reliability is when you are able to make and keep promises that only you know about. Self-reliability is the energy source for the Sexy + Soul-full woman's self-discipline, the power she infuses into her practice of the alchemy of time, making time for what she loves, unapologetically and joyfully. This is how she is able to do self-care and art, exercise her body and her creative side, envision her future and then actually follow through on her plans. This is one of the primary sources of the Sexy + Soul-full woman's confidence: She knows that she can plan, then trust in her ability to put her love into action. With self-reliability, all of her visioning and planning is infused with faith and trust.

Instead of focusing on external reliability, this chapter focuses almost exclusively on how to cultivate self-reliability. You will learn about how small acts of completion set the stage for larger, more significant efforts, which helps set apart the Sexy + Soul-full woman from her peers. By setting intentions, you'll gain greater self-respect—a gift that no one else can bestow upon you. By sharing your journey with a trusted other, you'll unleash the power of accountability.

ENJOYING COMPLETIONS

In putting together small acts of reliability and follow through, you're creating both a track record of completion as well as the foundation for building confidence in your own ability to do what you say you'll do. This string of kept promises is immeasurably important when it comes to doing more of what you love. Most often, your loves are your own. The doing of them is for yourself, for your own joy and delight. If you don't paint your canvas, finish the novel, take the acting class, run the 10K, lose the baby weight, or complete the degree, no one will be as disappointed as you. It may be that no one even knows or recognizes the absence of the completion—but you will know.

I understand this knowing of what's been left incomplete and undone. My past is littered with aspirations that were begun or imagined but never came to fruition. I've got a studio filled with art supplies from my previous flirtations with creativity. I have a lovingly restored antique fiddle that once belonged to an Arkansas jubilee fiddler, a fiddle I almost learned how to coax music from. I have two unfinished novels and dozens of characters wandering about in my imagination. If I'd not told you about them, you'd never know...yet, I've known about them for years, and the regret of these foundered efforts makes my heart ache and fills me with shame.

Shame is such a powerful force. It drives us into hiding and discourages the most important part of reliability: beginning again. Shame argues that after so many failures, making another attempt is pointless. That is not true. Beginning again is an act of hope and hope is an important ingredient in being reliable. Hope says that the future can be bright. Hope whispers that we can take steps toward tomorrow, one small, halting step at a time, gently placing our feet on faith. The path of hope is paved with small completions.

To become well versed in completion, to really enjoy and reap its benefits, you need to experience it over and over. Becoming fluent in small completions is a bit like flossing your teeth. One session of flossing is nice. Two in a row is better. A habit of flossing every day keeps your gums well cared for and reduces the build-up of plaque on your teeth. Like flossing, all little completions, every act of reliability, are small but sure steps toward a larger sense of trust in yourself. And when you have that trust in you, others will sense it and see it—and they will begin to trust you, too.

This is what it means to have self-reliability: You discern, set direction, and make commitments to yourself, and then you follow through on your commitments through actions. Self-reliability isn't an all or nothing. One day you wake up with it, and it's a yours forever kind of deal. It's created over time and, like just about everything, will be imperfect. That's okay. Being Sexy + Soul-full isn't about being perfect. It's about being resilient and persistent. Adversity will come—that much is certain—and you will get knocked down. But by practicing self-reliability, you will possess the knowledge that you can get up and go forward yet again.

SETTING INTENTIONS

One of the ways to cultivate reliability in yourself is by setting and keeping intentions. Intentions are different from milestones and actions. An intention is a word or phrase that expresses the way of being you want to keep in mind and to use to guide your decisions.

For example, when I promised myself to write this book, I set a small intention: no email and no social media until after I'd done my writing

The path of hope is paved with small completions.

for the day. I wanted to make my mornings into the most creative and effective part of each day. Like many of you, I carry my smart phone with me everywhere. And in a way, I have to: I'm on call 24-7 for my elderly mom. With that handy digital device always nearby, when I got stuck or fearful about my writing, I could immediately distract myself from my discomfort with Instagram or email. And once distracted, I found it very hard to come back to the source of discomfort: writing. So there were really two intentions: no email and no social media and breathe through the uncomfortable moments without running away from my work.

Each morning as I got out of bed, I chanted my intention like a mantra: "No email, no social media." Then I got right into my routine. When my writing was done, I made a note of how many words I produced, which was my way of marking each small completion. Contributing to the growing word count was also a tiny act of celebration as I saw the total increasing while creating an unbroken streak of days spent writing.

If I hadn't finished, only a few people besides me would have known my disappointment and regret of failing to keep my promise to myself. I would be the only one carrying the full weight of sadness of my unrealized potential and unshared gifts. That regret was a heaviness that I was just not willing to bear. My daily intentions encouraged me to withstand the temptations of email and social media and, instead, focus on the significant action of writing.

Making and keeping intentions can be your small acts of self-reliability that build your strength to carry out larger and larger completions. The trick, I believe, is keeping your eye on the process rather than the product or the outcome you'll produce when all is said and done. The magic is in the tiny step you'll take today, and then taking that tiny step, or one like it, again tomorrow and the day after. Frankly, I've come to distrust my imaginings of outcomes and what it'll be like when I'm done. Too often, I get enamored of the imagined praise and glory that I might receive—and that kind of validation becomes a temptation to me, wooing me away from the daily and present joy of setting and keeping my intentions.

"Divine love meets us in this real world, and nowhere else," writes Sister Ruth Burrows, "...in the daily round of seeming trivialities that afford no measure of self-glorification." This is exactly the nature of setting and keeping intentions. Small acts of self-reliability are sometimes so, so tedious. *Must I really cut little pieces of glass until my forearm aches and my hand cramps up?* Yes, if I want to complete a large, complex stained glass mosaic. *Must I really sand this entire door?* Yes, if you want it to look like the one you found on Pinterest. *Must I really sit down and write, even when I feel that I don't have anything to say, when I feel that I'm a fool for trying?* Yes, if you want the characters in your novel to come to life in the reader's imagination.

There is no self-glorification in the daily hard work of keeping your intentions to do your art, take your walk, count your calories, and all the hundred tiny acts of following through. There is no public adulation, no pats on the back, no recognition but your own. You know. And by being conscious of your efforts, noting your own follow through, you gain a respect for yourself that no one else can give you and no one can take away. As you've learned, mindfulness is a powerful means of noticing. This is another opportunity to put that power to use, noticing your efforts, the sincerity, persistence, and devotion required to keep trying.

When you fully comprehend your self-respect, even the most difficult and arduous climbs get just a little easier. Nurturing self-respect is part of how you can come to inhabit your own skin with comfort and ease:

- You believe in your own ability to take actions toward doing what you dream of doing.

- You become secure in your knowledge that you can conceive of an idea and carry it through to completion.

- You will have certainty because you've built your path of hope, paved with completion. Not that you will be perfect— no one is—but you will know that more often than not, you will come through.

- You will be able to trust yourself to be reliable.

Nurturing Accountability

Most often, it seems, people think of accountability as something negative. Partially this is due to the kind of accountability that they encounter in the workplace. In that case, a supervisor is bringing up some transgression and working with the employee to right the wrong. Those kinds of accountability conversations are often painful, frequently awkward, and sometimes punitive. However, the kind of accountability I'm encouraging you to use as a practitioner of Sexy + Soul-full Productivity is completely different from what you'll see in the workplace.

Sexy + Soul-full accountability is the simple act of owning up to what you did or didn't do. On a daily basis, you check in with yourself, reflect on how you're doing and what kind of progress you're making. You simply practice seeing what's there and stating that observation. No drama. No pissing and moaning. No self-aggrandizing. Simply: I made sincere effort in this area or I wasn't at my best and made no effort in another area. Objective self-awareness of your efforts is difficult to cultivate in solitude, however. To grow in keeping your promises to yourself, I advocate that you seek someone to be your partner in accountability. Seeing and saying what was or wasn't done are incandescent when practiced in the presence of another person. But not just any person—a person whom you can trust to be your witness, not your judge.

For this sort of shared accountability to work in your favor, it must become an act of both relationship and objectivity. Relationship because you are sharing with another person how you fared in your commitments to yourself and objectivity in that it's an exercise in stating what happened (or failed to happen) without squirming, apologizing, or making excuses. These two skills, observation and objectivity, go hand in hand to make accountability an efficacious practice in making and keeping promises to yourself.

I've had the privilege of watching these sorts of partnerships form as part of the coaching groups that I facilitate. One of my groups got the idea of using text messages to report in with each other between our monthly coaching sessions. What happened during this simple sharing was nothing short of miraculous. Dreams spoken in our coaching sessions were realized; failures were held with tenderness. We celebrated and mourned. We encouraged action and encountered fears. Each person participated with love and courage, bringing their daily offering of self. One year, a new member joined the already well-established group. She was reluctant to share her own daily accountings but willing to be witness for the others. Later, she told us that as she watched their exchanges, she felt braver. Her willingness to take risks, to go out on a limb, to reach farther than she thought she could—all grew. She felt enlivened by merely *watching* the process of accountability—even when she wasn't sharing her own story. This speaks to the nascent power of witnessing the journeys—both the triumphs and struggles—of others.

Accountability invites you forward, reminding you of why you wanted to make progress, what it is you're progressing toward.

How can something so ridiculously simple, the exchange of seeing and saying what was done or not done, be so powerful? When two (or more) are participating in this kind of accountability, the partnership creates an ambience of mutual encouragement. There is something deeply sacred in being present to each other's daily effort. When one is

189

struggling, the other is there to say, "Keep going." When one is joyful, the other is there to rejoice along with them. Yet there is also a lovely detachment—we are pulling for each other, yet have no stake in each other's outcomes. This objectivity creates an atmosphere of freedom in the encouraging. We are entirely "for" each other, yearning for each other's success and wellbeing, however that might come about or whatever it might consist of.

There is also a strong spiritual argument for sharing your struggles openly, with a trusted witness. When we keep our struggles, difficulties, and tribulations to ourselves, they fester. St. Ignatius of Loyola even went so far as to say that evil benefits from our isolation. "...when the enemy of human nature brings his wiles and persuasions to the just soul, he wants and desires that [the difficulties] be received and kept in secret..." Put another way, when desolation, doubt, and discouragement arrive, they much prefer to find you all alone so they have you to themselves.

Personally, I am very prone to spells of discouragement and desolation. Left to my own devices, I find it all too easy to "horrible-ize" about this and that. Before I know it, I'm having a pity party to which only I am invited where I play hide and seek with my fears and failures. No matter how well I hide, my fears and failures are incredibly adept at finding me!

When I keep all these troubles to myself, they seem to multiply with frightening rapidity. But when I drag myself out of hiding and into conversation with my friend, Augusto, he helps shine a light on possibility and hope. He reminds me of my past successes and emphasizes action over obsessing. Just by telling him what I did or didn't do, I begin to see my work with a different perspective—with less drama and more matter of factness. Just being in the presence of my loving witness makes me want to be better: a better person, a better writer, a better witness for his journey so that I can reciprocate the gift his companionship has given me. He imagines his own dreams and discerns his own direction, as I do mine, and together, in conversation, week after week, year after year, we walk our paths, reminding each other of what we're about. I can point to many completions which would never have happened without Augusto's encouragement; he can do the same.

This is what accountability does: It invites you forward, reminding you of why you wanted to make progress, what it is you're progressing toward. And at the same time, you're in community, in relationship, helping someone else just as they are helping you. Most importantly, though, the act of accounting what you did or didn't do puts you in repeated contact with your efforts and actions—the ones you took and the ones you didn't take. Additively, it is your actions that lead to completions and focusing on the actions themselves allows you to immerse yourself in process and dismiss, for the time being, product.

The work is sometimes plodding, often halting and shaky, a step at a time. And then another. And another. Your book doesn't suddenly leap into existence; the completed work is forged from the raw materials you hunt and gather and glean. Your screenplay is hammered together, a phrase here, a scene there, a perfectly emitted sound that tells a story better than a thousand lines of dialog could. No one need be there with you, not even your loyal accountability partner, when you're waiting with the camera until your fingers go numb, waiting for the exact moment when the hummingbird alights on the flower and you snap the photo. But witnessing your doing as you cobble together each mundane, seemingly trivial action, accountability marks the progress that leads to that moment of victory, however small.

If indeed you want to do more of what you love, then accountability is one of your most valuable skills. Both in the speaking of your own doing and the witnessing of someone else's. You become for one another the objective observer who yearns for each other's success yet has no stake in the outcome. This loving, detached, compassionate objectivity provides a sure and steady feedback that bears no resemblance to praise or criticism. It's the reply to your heart's longing when you ask the question, "What's it going to take? What must I do to move forward?"

Mutual accountability, however, can only take you so far. To take full possession of your own self-reliability, you must learn to be accountable to yourself alone. For this, I suggest you begin practicing a daily review I'm calling the Soul-full Examen.

The original Examen was set out as a form of prayer for those who practice Ignatian Spirituality. Your Soul-full Examen will be slightly different from the traditional prayer form (although the two can be easily merged if you wish). In both, the intention is to review the day and glean loving insights that are implemented the following day.

EXERCISE

Here are the steps for undertaking a Soul-full Examen.

1. At the end of your day, quiet yourself and find the place of stillness in your heart—the same place of stillness from which your discernment came. Look on yourself and your day with the perspective of love.

2. Recall the gifts you experienced during the day and offer gratitude for each one.

3. Call to mind what your plan was for the day: What did you intend to do? In what areas had you planned to invest your efforts? With love, ask yourself which areas received sincere and devoted effort and which did not. Simply observe your responses and accept each one with love and compassion.

4. In stillness, forgive yourself for any times when you were unable to give your best effort regardless of the reason why. When you see that you were effortful, no matter how effective those efforts were, give yourself the gift of thanks.

5. Looking ahead, consider how to bring your most sincere and devoted effort to bear on the day to come. Make plans accordingly.

6. Conclude your Examen with prayer, silent meditation, or by reading from a source of wisdom and encouragement.

No matter how sincere and devoted your efforts, all actions yield results. In the final chapter of this section on putting love into action, we will consider how to receive your results with grace.

chapter eleven

Receiving Results with Grace

By NOW, YOU are probably aware that you cannot control how your efforts turn out nor how they are judged by others. Because life's roller coaster ride is so variable, learning how to receive your results with grace is an essential skill. Commonly, the way your efforts turn out are labelled as successes and failures. The Sexy + Soul-full perspective is, as usual, a little different. Instead, I encourage you to receive *all* your results with grace.

How Do You Receive?

Cultivating humility is the first step in receiving results with grace.

Often, frustratingly so, your results are out of your hands. This is one of the hardest truths of life to bear. You work hard, dammit! Yet, deep down, you know that you can do all the right things, take all the proper steps, make sincere and devoted effort, yet not receive the results you intended. On the flip side, sometimes you get exactly what you aimed for, and that's a time for joy and celebration. Ultimately, however, both kinds of results, the ones you wanted and the ones you didn't, can be received with the same grace.

You've already learned about equanimity, an attitude of composure—a calmness, a steadiness—that remains centered and stable in the face of whatever comes along, good or bad. This composure, paired

One of the simplest and quickest paths to humility is to cultivate the ability to celebrate other people's accomplishments as if those were your own.

with humility, allows you to receive your results as gifts and welcome them gracefully no matter what form they take. Whether you are blessed with fruitful triumph or have met a dismal dead end, with grace, you will not be blown up or blown away. The center of you, your essential self, remains intact and whole. When paired with humility, equanimity becomes a powerful tool for maintaining courage regardless of your circumstances or how your efforts are turning out.

From a spiritual point of view, a balanced perspective on results is incredibly important. Obtaining negative results or coming up short can drive us down and discourage us terribly. I know this kind of disappointment from repeated experience. Not only has not getting what I wanted been hard on my heart, I often find myself feeling jealous of those that I believe are getting what I wanted for myself. Jealousy, which is born of comparison, turns my heart away from love and toward bitterness and hatred. Attachment to positive results is equally dangerous. Arrogance, addiction to accomplishment, perfectionism, and feelings of entitlement may trail in the wake of being too fond of positive results. Humility is the answer to avoiding all of these problems.

One of the simplest and quickest paths to humility is to cultivate the ability to celebrate other people's accomplishments as if those were your own. Trust me, I know how difficult it can be to smile and genuinely say, "Congratulations!" to someone when I would rather jump to jealousy instead. One of the greatest indicators of a person's true character, however, is how she responds to hearing praise—not praise she receives, but praise of others! The woman who is uncomfortable in her own skin seethes when she hears another person receiving accolades. I know how she feels because, often, I've felt the same way. One of the milestones of progress for me is that I am now more able to feel joyful for another when I see her doing well. The great spiritual writer, Thomas à Kempis, put it this way, "Whatever goodness or virtue is in you, believe that your neighbor has better qualities. It will not hurt you to consider [her to be better than yourself] even if this is not really so... A humble person is a peaceful person..." And to peaceful, I would add Sexy + Soul-full, as well.

Naturally, negative results or lack of progress are harder to receive than positive results or joyful completions are. Yet, by remaining humble and residing with equanimity, both can be met with grace. There is a beautiful poem by Rumi which explains this much better than I ever could:

> This being human is a guest house.
> Every morning a new arrival.
> A joy, a depression, a meanness,
> Some momentary awareness comes
> As an unexpected visitor.

Rumi encourages us to simply receive them all, with exactly the same kind of hospitality and grace, no matter how lovely or how ugly the visitor might be. "Be grateful for whatever comes," says Rumi, "because each has been sent as a guide from beyond."

What Are You Grateful For?

The second step in receiving results with grace is to receive them with gratitude.

I owe my discovery of gratitude to Sarah Ban Breathnach, the author of *Simple Abundance: A Daybook of Comfort and Joy*. It was she who pointed me to the simple practice of looking for five things for which I am thankful and faithfully writing those down every evening. I read her book in 1995 and began keeping a simple gratitude journal right away. Now, twenty years later, I am still recording my gratitude every single night before I turn out the light and go to sleep.

This simple ritual of gratitude has fundamentally changed me. During the writing of this book, for example, there were so many times when completion seemed far away, out of reach, or completely impossible. Progress was invisible. My effort was flagging. My enthusiasm waned. But gratitude re-energized me and pulled me through. Most importantly, it reconnected me with the essentials: the warmth of the sun on my skin, the feeling of my dog's fur under my hand, the laughter over coffee when my husband spontaneously sings "Do Ya Think I'm Sexy?" to make me laugh. Those were the experiences that lightened my days while toiling away. If I hadn't been alert to them, recording their occurrences, chances are, they'd have been lost.

"Sunlight is what changes the openness of a [lotus bloom]. The openness of our minds and hearts obey the warmth of positivity," says Barbara Fredrickson, luminary in the field of positive psychology. Unlike the study of the pathology of the human mind, positive psychology focuses on the best of human functioning, seeking to improve what works. Fredrickson's research has illuminated how gratitude, along with other positive emotions, create spaciousness within us. The experience of positive emotions creates the ability to feel *more* positive emotion. Even better, this ability becomes an enduring strength, or as Frederickson puts it, a "lasting cognitive resource." In other words, gratitude builds on itself to make more permanent changes within you.

"Be grateful for whatever comes," says Rumi, "because each has been sent as a guide from beyond."

There are many ways to engage with gratitude but I have found two approaches that seem to work the best.

The first is to keep a gratitude journal, as I mentioned earlier. At the end of each day, write down five things that you are grateful for. Often, during my darkest hours, it was this glimmer of gratitude that kept me going, looking for just five things I could point to and be thankful for. When I miscarried my one and only pregnancy, I was thankful for cards and flowers, prayers, and sunlight. After my dad died, I found gratitude in long walks, phone calls from friends, and quiet at the end of really difficult days; sometimes, I was just grateful that the day was over. I learned that every day, no matter how awful, still comes with gifts—and the best response to receiving a gift is to say "Thank you."

The second practice is called the "Three Good Things Exercise." The idea is that you note three good things that happened to you and then identify what action you took or what choice you made that allowed you to experience that "good thing." You don't need to take on the Three Good Things exercise permanently; most folks use it for just five to seven days in a row to experience its infusion of gratitude goodness.

Kristin came to me for coaching because she hated her job. During her very first session, I suggested the Three Good Things exercise. When she returned, a week later, the change was nothing short of miraculous. She was discovering more than three good things everyday—and some of them were at work! Her perspective on her job changed so dramatically that she ended up remaining with her company until her husband's career led them to a different city.

Whichever practice you choose as your own, gratitude helps you to see that you owe so much of your life to the world around you. Gratitude also reminds you of how much you have, which harkens back to your earlier apprenticeship to enough. While "my time is precious," with the unspoken "and yours is not," leads you to overvalue your own experiences, gratitude allows you to see how relationships provide your life with their greatest treasures. Because you have enough, you can be more generous with your time—which is another way of expressing gratitude. Gratitude, like stillness, is a great antidote to impatience, irritation, and urgency, all three of which are fed by three destructive myths about time that you worked so hard to reject earlier.

WHEN DO YOU CELEBRATE?

The third step in receiving results with grace is celebration.

Positive results wouldn't be complete without celebration. Celebrating isn't just a pat on the back or gaining recognition. If fact, those are the least of the benefits that celebration bestows on you. Celebration is the act of taking possession of, and owning, your experiences. It is by naming and being present to your completions, you gain knowledge of what you are good at and the value of your effort. Only by understanding and recognizing the worth of your work can you be in full ownership of what you do and be ready to stand up for yourself.

What does celebration consist of? In the simplest form, celebration can be a pause, a moment, a smile, a flower in the vase on your desk. Celebration can be a massage, a good book, or a glass of wine raised in a toast to the significance of something only you know. Celebration might arrive as a line in your gratitude journal. You can celebrate by enrolling in a class you've been wanting to take, basking in an afternoon spent on your art, taking a walk alone so you can hear your own voice and sing your own praises to yourself, your muses, and to whomever else you wish to share your joy. Of course, celebrations can be lavish, too. There's nothing like a good party and some champagne to mark a significant celebration!

By celebrating your milestones, you bring your completions with you, a treasure trove that you can draw from wherever you go. It's said that women are poor negotiators for their own benefit, gaining (on average) fewer raises and bonuses than men who do the same work. As a Sexy + Soul-full woman who knows how to celebrate, you are in a better position to argue on your own behalf and bolder in doing so because you understand the value of your abilities, the worth of your completions, and the advantages you bring to your employers or collaborators.

Celebration, like receiving your results, includes humility. You know that your accomplishments are earned by your efforts, not owed to you by entitlement. Give credit to yourself, yes, but also share credit generously with others. This sharing is a natural extension of gratitude, a way of offering your work and completions to a greater power than your own. A rising tide, after all, lifts all boats. When you make progress, you make it possible for others to progress, to surpass their own limitations, to gain greater freedom and seek new possibilities. This is part of how celebration nurtures your inner strength and confidence.

Celebration of reaching milestones, in joy and with humility, can also supply the understanding you need to let go of external validation. You are perfectly capable of giving yourself approval, seeing yourself and what you do with love. This ability to supply yourself with approval makes external validation irrelevant and unnecessary. And thus, when recognition from the outside comes to you, it's a blessing that only adds to your already bountiful sense of celebration.

Last, but certainly not least, celebration allows you a chance to savor the sweetness of completion, being fully present for it, reaping joy and fulfillment from your work. Without this kind of pause, however brief, your work may feel endless. But with even modest celebration, energy and light are restored and purpose and meaning are recalled. Those reminders of the deeper reasons for your efforts are what will help keep you loyal to your journey, even when the going is tough and completions are far apart, or when adversity looms or storm clouds gather.

WHEN DO YOU QUIT?

I would be remiss in not addressing the possibility of failure. What if you undertake sincere and devoted effort, yet cannot reach the significant milestones that signal expected progress? If you encounter only negative results, when do you admit that it's time to quit?

First, you must distinguish dead-end from discouragement.

A dead end is the true end of a journey. At a dead end, there is no place to go except to admit that the pursuit of the calling, whatever that was, isn't going to be realized. Going back to the example of becoming a yoga teacher, the inability to complete the required coursework, even after repeated attempts and much sincere and devoted effort, could be a dead end. In the case of a true and obvious dead end, you would be free to reenter discernment and seek another direction or calling.

You are perfectly capable of giving yourself approval, seeing yourself and what you do with love.

Discouragement, however, can look like a dead end but is not necessarily an indication of failure. Discouragement is the loss of love, warmth, peace, and joy in your work. When discouraged, feelings of frustration, fatigue, self-doubt, worry, and anxiety cloud your perspective on how you're doing. For this reason, please don't quit while in the grips of discouragement! Instead, take the time to carefully assess the causes of your feelings.

Discouragement can naturally follow from genuine physical causes. Stress, circumstances, and even the weather can drive our moods and push our feelings toward discouragement. While writing the first draft of this book, I had a day when I felt incredibly positive and optimistic. The following day, I was so grumpy and discouraged that I thought about quitting. The only difference between the two days was the weather! My moods can be very tied to sunshine and exercise. Address those simple solutions first before considering whether or not you're meant to give up.

There is another kind of spiritual discouragement that has a much deeper root and goes by the name "desolation." Desolation is a dryness of the soul that may include confusion, hopelessness, and loss of faith. When I've been in the throes of desolation, I've questioned everything about myself from my talents and abilities to my reason for living. One of the hallmarks of desolation is that there seems to be no precipitating cause. The darkness of desolation shows up out of nowhere and saps all traces of energy away.

Above all else, resist desolation. Talk about your feelings with a trusted friend, your pastor, a coach, or someone else who can hear you without trying to fix you. Seek encouragement; you may not believe the encouragement you receive when in desolation (I didn't) but you need to hear

During desolation, your job is to cultivate hope, remain loyal to your direction, continue your efforts, and trust that desolation will pass.

it anyway. And fight back by engaging hope. Hope is not always an emotion—it can also be a way of thinking.

Desolation is characterized by thoughts of hopelessness. Hope gives you a way up and out of desolation through revisiting direction (which you received during your discernment), adhering to your plan (the one you constructed in chapter on "Taking Vision Into Action"), and reminding yourself of your ability to do what you set out to do (which you cultivated in learning self-reliability). Sticking to your plans is vitally important during periods of desolation. This is not to say that you might change your plans later, but *not* while in desolation. During desolation, your job is to cultivate hope, remain loyal to your direction, continue your efforts, and trust that desolation will pass.

Once you regain a sense of peace and begin to experience periods characterized by a sense of well-being (which some spiritual writers refer to as consolation), you can assess your situation and consider whether or not you are ready to stop trying. Not to be repetitive, but, again, quitting should *never* be considered during times of discouragement and desolation! You are not in an objective frame of mind and cannot discern if you've failed when you are in the grips of a "dark night of the soul."

Assuming that you are in a good frame of mind and have your wits about you, and you have not reached an obvious dead end, here are some simple guidelines for making a decision about quitting.

1. In times when you are truly centered, feeling a sense of peace and joy, what is your inclination toward continuing? Inclination means the course of action you are attracted to take. Like discernment of direction, inclination is a response of your heart and needs no explanations or rationales.

2. Consider what form of action expresses your deepest and most authentic sense of who you are as a person. Even in the face of almost certain failure, continuing may be a better option. Among the great women of history are dozens of examples of staying the course even when the challenges were insurmountable. Blessed Teresa of Calcutta, better known as

Mother Teresa, knew she couldn't conquer the poverty of those she served but that did nothing to stop her from providing care to thousands of suffering people during her lifetime.

3. Evaluate the advantages and disadvantages to quitting. Personally, I use a "four-quadrant" form that pits costs and pay-offs against quitting or not-quitting. I evaluate each combination: the cost of quitting, the cost of not-quitting, the pay-off of quitting, the pay-off of not-quitting. More often than not, the scale tips very naturally in one direction (quitting or not quitting).

If, after careful consideration, you decide to quit, there is no shame in making an ending nor does quitting mean that your discernment about your original direction was wrong. You obtained results from your actions as all actions produce results. Results are a bit like icebergs. Most of an iceberg is underwater and invisible from above. Results, too, are mostly unseen. You really have no idea what you've accomplished and the effects your actions may have had! By taking sincere and devoted effort and putting your love into action, you can trust that you were a positive influence in the world, even if you never see those effects.

Conclusion

Tonight, I'll open a bottle of champagne to toast the completion of our journey together. We've covered a lot of ground! And now, you're ready to venture forth into whatever your soul is being called toward.

As you pack your bags, you have many new skills and abilities to take with you. You've completed three apprenticeships that, with continued practice, will yield mastery in the alchemy of time. From your discernment of direction, you will be able to navigate through the choppy waters of life's storms and sail over glassy seas when the wind is at your back and everything is going your way. You've got plans based on realities and centered on your loves. And you have the strengths of self-reliability and grace to receive your results. Yes, you are very well equipped for whatever your future may hold. Yet, I have one last gift for you: my heart.

My heart is along with you no matter where your path leads. I will be your invisible companion, your unseen encourager. Even though your future may be uncertain, I know that risking security for a life well-loved is a worthy undertaking. You can always be certain that my heart is close to yours as you follow your soul's deepest callings.

Your adventure is just beginning! May every step you take be blessed.

ACKNOWLEDGMENTS

This book could never have been written without the love and encouragement of my husband, Douglas. He has always believed in me in ways I could never have hoped to believe in myself. I am always so amazed at his confidence in me. It's my hope to reward his faith by becoming and being the person he thinks I am: talented, capable, confident, and creative. Thank you, sweet boy, for everything you've done with and for me for the past twenty-something years of our lives. I love you far beyond anything I'll ever be able to express.

My mom has been a constant source of love for me. Her enthusiasm for my writing knows no bounds. She's waited a long time to read this book. I hope it brings her joy and delight to see its completion. Mama, you are such an inspiration to me; I am so grateful for your prayers and your companionship.

An entire community of friends, clients, podcast listeners, and readers sent me messages of hope and inspiration through the past year. At the risk of leaving someone out, I owe especially big hugs and debts of gratitude to Suzanne Austin-Bythell, Augusto Pinaud, Brenda Gregory, James Lamkin, Otis Henderson, Barb and Chris Anderson, Silvina de Brum, Pam King, Jodi Kilcup, Gaylie Cashman, Sunia Yang, Carissa Cousins, Daniel Gold, and Heather King.

This book came to fruition with the assistance of numerous professionals. Heather King edited the first draft of the manuscript with finesse and skill. Judie Harvey was my editorial angel through the completion of the manuscript—her enthusiasm, encouragement, and professionalism gave me the energy I needed and calmed my anxiety. My vocabulary is inadequate to express my thanks to Michael Kastre of St. Michael's Press and his team of graphic art and layout professionals, Hedeer El-Showk and Veronica El-Showk.

So many authors and thought leaders contributed their wisdom. Among the most important influencers in my journey, I want to thank Brené Brown, whose work literally changed my life. Brené's wisdom, humor, and vulnerability gave me the courage to write this book. Tara Mohr taught a wonderful course called Playing Big, which gave me a huge push in the right direction. I've mentioned Lynne Twist repeatedly throughout the book, and I thank her again now. Poet David Whyte's voice accompanied me for hours while driving and exercising; I am so grateful for his words, which strengthened my resolve to have the courageous conversation with life. Both Kelly Rae Roberts (*Taking Flight: Inspiration and Techniques to Give Your Creative Spirit Wings*) and Jennifer Lee (*The Right-Brained Business Plan: A Creative, Visual Map for Success*) gave me lots of joy, energy, and creative inspiration.

Finally, I thank God. My faith continues to be the most important source of strength and love for me. May all the glory be yours!

About the Author

Tara Rodden Robinson, Ph.D., is a coach, author, and artist. She founded her coaching practice in 2006 when she left a career in academia. Before becoming a coach, she enjoyed a lively adventure as a biologist beginning in the Costa Rican rainforest. While pursuing her Ph.D. at the University of Illinois (Urbana-Champaign), she met and married her soul mate, W. Douglas Robinson. Tara has published numerous papers on tropical birds and is the author of *Genetics for Dummies* (Wiley), now in its second edition. Before becoming a biologist, Tara earned her bachelor's degree in nursing and she practiced critical care and surgical nursing for five years.

Tara's mission is to empower, equip, and encourage individuals and organizations so that they are freed to better contribute their talents, strengths, and gifts to the world at large.

Tara makes her home in Corvallis, Oregon, where she lives in a purple house surrounded by art. She finds joy in making mosaics, painting in mixed-media, binding books, practicing yoga, or hiking the forest trails with her husband and their dog, Rowdy.

To learn about Tara's coaching, workshops, art, and more, visit tararobinson.com.

Notes

Preface

Augusto Pinaud: An accomplished author in his own right, you can learn more about Augusto by visiting his website, http://augustopinaud.com.

Introduction

Getting Things Done: David Allen. *Getting Things Done: The Art of Stress-free Productivity* (Penguin Books, 2002).

Twice-monthly podcast: You can listen to back episodes of the GTD Virtual Study Group by visiting www.gtd-vsg. blogspot.com

Traits of masculinity: The traits of masculinity were drawn from the work of James R. Mahalik and his colleagues who studied masculine gender role norms in U.S. society. Mahalik et al. included that "control over women" and violence were also considered important attributes of being a man in the United States. See James R. Mahalik, et al. 2003. Development of the conformity to masculine norms inventory. *Psychology of Men & Masculinity* 1:3-25.

4   **Christiane Northrup:** I first encountered Dr. Christiane Northrup when I read her book, *Women's Bodies, Women's Wisdom: Creating Physical and Emotional Health and Healing* (Bantam, 1994). Any woman who wants to better understand her body and its rhythms, or any man who wants to understand the female experience, may find the book a helpful resource.

4   **Our culture expects women to put others first…:** This quote is drawn from Christiane Northrup, M.D. *The Wisdom of Menopause: Creating Emotional and Physical Health During the Change, Revised Edition* (Bantam, 2012). The emphasis in italics is hers. The quote is at Location 332 of the Kindle version.

5   **Desired outcomes as the definition of success…:** "I define "success" as achieving desired results or experience," David Allen, quoted on April 30, 2010 on the Getting Things Done - Official GTD Page on Facebook, http://goo.gl/DJCWTy.

6   **"You are not enough.":** Brené Brown writes about our cultural obsession with "not enough" and the shame it causes, in her book, *The Gifts of Imperfection: Let Go of Who You Think You're Supposed to Be and Embrace Who You Are* (Hazelden, 2010).

6   **"More is always better.":** See Chapter 3, "Scarcity: The Great Lie" in Lynne Twist. *The Soul of Money: Reclaiming the Wealth of Our Inner Resources.* (W.W. Norton & Company, 2003).

6   **The work world, which is dominated by men:** Even though women make up nearly 47% of the workforce and occupy 51% of management positions, they earn less than men do, on average, and are less likely to be in positions of corporate leadership. Less than 5% of CEO and other executive positions are held by women. See Catalyst. *Pyramid: Women in S&P 500 Companies.* New York: Catalyst, January 13, 2015; http://www.catalyst.org/knowledge/women-sp-500-companies. For statistics and sources: Ariane Hegewisch, Williams, C., Harbin, V. 2012. The gender wage gap by occupation. *Institute for Women's Policy Research* IWPR publication #C350a; http://www.iwpr.org/publications/pubs/the-gender-wage-gap-by-occupation-1/.

8   **Walking for just forty minutes three times a week:** This study, conducted on older adults, was aimed at assessing how brain connectivity is affected by exercise. Connectivity typically worsens as we age but walking seemed to mitigate these effects. See Michelle W. Voss, et al. 2010. Plasticity of brain networks in a randomized intervention trial of exercise training in older adults. *Frontiers in Aging Neuroscience* 2:32. doi: 10.3389/fnagi.2010.00032

8   **Other studies show:** These and many more examples of the power of exercise to improve brain function generally, and productivity specifically, can be found in John J. Ratey, Jr., M.D. and Hagerman, E. *Spark: The Revolutionary New Science of Exercise and the Brain* (Little, Brown, and Company, 2008).

8   **Four hours of cardio:** Sharon Toker and Biron, M. 2012. Job burnout and depression: Unraveling their temporal relationship and considering the role of physical activity. *Journal of Applied Psychology* 97:699-710; http://psycnet.apa.org/doi/10.1037/a0026914.

8   **How our bodies and minds interact:** If you need proof of my contention about women and the body-mind connection, take a look at the sex ratio in your next yoga class. Yoga emphasizes that mind-body connection as an integral part of practice, and I'm guessing you'll see many more women than men in most yoga studios, just as I have.

9   **The intimate roles of life:** Intimate here means private as opposed to public. These would be roles like mother, wife, soulmate, partner, friend, daughter, sister.

9   **Nurturing is a key word for us women:** As opposed to fight-or-flight, women tend-and-befriend. See Shelley E. Taylor,. et al. 2000. Biobehavioral responses to stress in females: Tend-and-befriend not fight-or-flight. *Psychological Review* 107: 411-429.

10   **For those who have eyes to see and ears to hear…:** David G. Benner. *Spirituality and the Awakening Self: The Sacred Journey of Transformation.* (Brazos Press, 2012). Quote is at Location 417 of the Kindle version.

11   **An inclusive approach:** To accomplish this, I keep "God-language" to a minimum and use words like "the Divine" and "spirit" instead. My goal is to make the book accessible to all readers, regardless of their spiritual traditions (or lack thereof).

11   **Exploring the mystical:** I understand mysticism as a direct, personal experience of the Divine or a direct encounter with "ultimate Truth." There are many forms of mysticism including Buddhist, Christian, Hindu, and Islamic traditions. Evelyn Underhill defined mysticism as the "science or art of the spiritual life." See Evelyn Underhill. *Mysticism: A Study in Nature and Development of Spiritual Consciousness.*(12th ed.; Evinity Publishing, 2009) [original publication date 1911].

(Re)Discovering What You Love

13   **Owning our story:** Brown, *Gifts of Imperfection;* Kindle loc 63.

The Archaeology of the Soul

16   **Like archaeologists of the soul:** As best I can tell, this quote

is drawn from *Caroline Myss' Journal of Inner Dialogue*. I found the quote in a blog post by Kelly Rae Roberts but the source was not included. See http://kellyraeroberts. blogspot.com/2013/03/yes-to-growing-yes-to-healing.html

17 **Federal court order in 1967:** "Desegregate schools in '67, 6 states told." *Chicago Tribune,* March 30, 1967; http:// archives.chicagotribune.com/1967/03/30/page/7/article/ desegregate-schools-in-67-6-states-told

17 **Mrs. Lakeshore:** Name withheld to protect her privacy.

17 **A chicken hawk:** Chicken hawk is southern vernacular for Red-tailed Hawk *(Buteo jamaicensis).* Despite how this tale turned out, I still feel an especial love and affinity for this particular bird of prey.

18 **Shame:** Shame is such a powerful and long-lasting force that I actually felt it again while recalling and writing this section. Brené Brown's books on this topic are rich sources for understanding the role that shame can play in our lives. Her work on being wholehearted changed my life.

19 **Give my life to Christ:** The religion of my upbringing emphasized a personal decision for conversion. By declaring my desire to give my life to Christ, I "got saved," as Evangelical Protestants put it. Baptism by immersion typically follows.

19 **Mary Slavant:** This is her actual name. She is deceased.

23 **Ouachita High School:** Ouachita is pronounced "WASH-i-taw."

24 **Ouachita Parish:** Instead of counties, Louisiana is organized into parishes. This centuries-old custom dates back to the time when the region belonged to France.

27 **Northeast Louisiana University:** Northeast, also known as NLU, is now called University of Louisiana, Monroe.

28 **Gary:** Name changed to protect privacy.

The Doors to the World of the Soul-full Self

33 **The doors to the world:** Clarissa Pinkola Estés, Ph.D. *Women Who Run with Wolves: Myths and Stories of the Wild Woman Archetype* (Ballentine Books, 1992). Quote is found on p 21.

33 **Brains don't fully mature until our late twenties:** In truth, the human brain continues to develop and change throughout life. Gray matter density (GMD) seems to peak in the late-20's or early 30's. GMD is the portion of the brain that is responsible for self-control and decision making functions, among others. See Elizabeth R. Sowell, et al. (2003) Mapping cortical change across the human life span. *Nature Neuroscience* 6:309-315 and citations therein.

34 **She must learn:** Granted, there are male nurses but nursing is still a primarily female profession. As nurses, women

outnumber men dramatically. According to the U.S. Census, in 2011, there were 3.5 million nurses employed in the United States, only 330,000 of whom were male. See Liana C. Landivar. 2013. Men in Nursing Occupations. United States *Census Bureau Highlight Report*. http://www.census.gov/people/io/files/Men_in_Nursing_Occupations.pdf

35 **Tropical regions are home:** A.G. Fischer. 1961. Latitudinal variations in organic diversity. *American Scientist* 49:50-74.

36 **Rara Avis:** Rara Avis, which means "rare bird," is an incredible rainforest lodge and preserve, founded by Amos Bien. You can learn more by visiting their website: http://www.rara-avis.com/.

38 **GRE:** Graduate Record Exam. The GRE is the standardized entrance exam required by most graduate schools.

40 **Department of Ecology, Ethology, and Evolution:** My home department of graduate studies has since been reorganized as the School of Integrative Biology. Ethology is an old term for the field of study of animal behavior.

42 **Song Wrens:** Tara Rodden Robinson. 2000. *Factors affecting natal dispersal by Song Wrens (Cyphorhinus phaeocephalus): Ecological constraints and demography*. Ph.D. dissertation. University of Illinois, Urbana.

42 **Lisa:** Name changed to protect privacy of her family.

43 **Chances of having a baby at age thirty-eight:** Loss of fecundity begins at around age 31. See B.M. van Noord-Zaadstra et al. 1991. Delaying childbearing: effect of age on fecundity and outcome of pregnancy. *British Medical Journal* 302:1361-1365.

43 **Like all women over thirty-five:** See D. Navot et al. 1991. Poor oocyte quality rather than implantation failure as a cause of age-related decline in female fertility. *The Lancet* 337: 1375-1377.

45 **The Vajra:** The shop and its prayer wheel are a Capitol Hill landmark. You can visit them next time you're in Seattle, Washington, at 518 Broadway East.

The Unraveling at Midlife

47 **People may call:** Brown, *Gifts of Imperfection;* Kindle loc 127.

49 **The departmental strategic plan:** At the time, I had little experience with strategic planning. Since then, I've learned that organizations don't normally form strategy around particular individuals.

49 **No matter what you do:** As an aside, the other faculty spouse, the one who was named in the strategic plan, was later hired.

52 **A professional who works with people:** The International

Coach Federation defines coaching as: "Partnering with clients in a thought-provoking and creative process that inspires them to maximize their personal and professional potential... Coaches honor the client as the expert in his or her life and work and believe every client is creative, resourceful and whole."

56 **Called to start running:** Kelly Rae Roberts. *Taking Flight: Inspiration and Techniques to Give Your Creative Spirit Wings* (North Light Books, 2008). Kelly's story about "the loudest, pesky whisper" is on p 12.

57 **If you are ever in any way discouraged:** Francis de Sales. *St. Francis de Sales: Selected Letters* (De Sales Resources and Ministries, 2011). From a letter written to Soeur de Bréchard on 22 July 1616; quote is found on p 246.

59 **Author Byron Katie:** Byron Katie. *Loving What Is: Four Questions that Can Change Your Life.* (Harmony, 2002).

60 **Committed:** Elizabeth Gilbert. *Committed: A Love Story.* (Penguin Books, 2011).

60 **Eat, Pray, Love:** Elizabeth Gilbert. *Eat, Pray, Love: One Woman's Search for Everything Across Italy, India and Indonesia.* (Penguin Books, 2007).

60 **In her own words:** This story was drawn "What to Do If You Can't Find Your Passion," by Eiizabeth Gilbert published in *O: The Oprah Magazine* (accessed online: http://www.

oprah.com/spirit/Elizabeth-Gilbert-on-the-Importance-of-Curiosity)

61   **In her prayer:** Heather King. *Shirt of Flame: A Year with Saint Thérèse of Lisieux* (Paraclete Press, 2011). Quote is found on p 79.

Make Time for What You Love

63   **Lynne Twist:** Twist, *The Soul of Money;* Kindle loc 674.

Three Destructive Myths About Time

68   **Alicia:** Name changed to protect privacy.

70   **The "yes-damn" phenomenon:** While I discovered the yes-damn from personal experience, the phrase was coined by Gal Zauberman and John Lynch in their research paper on time discounting and resource slack. "Slack" is the imagined surplus of any given resource, in this case, time. Their research showed that people over-estimate slack for future time but don't make the same mistake when thinking about money. See G. Zauberman, G. and Lynch, J.G., Jr. 2005. Resource slack and propensity to discount delayed investments of time versus money. *Journal of Experimental Psychology: General* 134: 23-37

71   **Resource slack:** Ibid.

71   **People put off all kinds of things:** The tendency to

procrastinate on enjoyable experiences is an excellent example of just how insidious the myth of "more time later" really is. This subject has been well studied by Professors Suzanne Shu and Ayelet Gneezy. See their paper S.B. Shu and Gneezy, A. 2010. Procrastination of enjoyable experiences. *Journal of Marketing Research* 47: 933-944. doi: http://dx.doi.org/10.1509/jmkr.47.5.933

71   **Rodney Smith:** Rodney Smith. 2010. "Undivided mind: Becoming whole." *Tricycle: The Buddhist Review* Summer 2010. Accessed online August 14, 2010.

72   **Leaning toward or away:** Ibid.

72   **We cannot delay:** Ibid.

72   **St. Ignatius of Loyola:** St. Ignatius possessed a keen understanding of human psychology and was centuries ahead of his time in how he understood emotions as part of the spiritual life. This particular piece of advice appears in his letter to the Community at Alcala. W.J. Young (Translator). *Letters of St. Ignatius of Loyola.* (Loyola Press, 1959) p. 441. Accessed online via Google Books.

73   **Acedia:** I first learned about acedia from Kathleen Norris' book, *Acedia and Me: A marriage, monks, and a writer's life* (Riverhead, 2008). She gives a detailed history of the concept, as well as a helpful exploration of the difference between acedia and depression.

73 **Nihilism:** A post-modern philosophy, nihilism posits that life is without meaning or purpose.

74 **Time may not actually exist at all:** The most recent thinking on this topic hypothesizes that the universe may be a holographic projection. There's a long article in the uber-respectable scientific journal, *Nature,* that explains all the current understanding of space and time. If after reading the article, you understand how the universe works, please explain it to me: Zeeya Merali. 2013. Theoretical physics: The origins of space and time. *Nature* 500: 516-519.

74 **Everything that has happened:** This idea is still quite controversial but in a weird kind of spiritual way, it makes sense to me. You can learn more about the hypothesis that "everything is now" and its originator here: Adam Frank. 2012. "There is no such thing as time." *Popular Science Online* http://www.popsci.com/science/article/2012-09/book-excerpt-there-no-such-thing-time

75 **Time is this rubbery thing:** David Eagleman's story—of how he got interested in the way time works, his research methods, and his viewpoints on life in general—is absolutely fascinating. The quote was drawn from G. Bilger. 2011. "The Possibilian." *The New Yorker,* April 25, 2011. Accessed online: http://www.newyorker.com/reporting/2011/04/25/110425fa_fact_bilger?currentPage=all.

75 **The less information:** Ibid.

76 **Truthy:** Derivative form of the word, "truthiness," coined by comedian Steven Colbert. Truthiness "is a quality characterizing a 'truth' that a person making an argument or assertion claims to know intuitively 'from the gut' or because it 'feels right' without regard to evidence, logic, intellectual examination, or facts." See http://en.wikipedia.org/wiki/Truthiness for examples.

78 **One clever study:** E.H. O'Brien, Anastasio, P.A., and Bushman, B.J. 2011. Time crawls when you're not having fun: Feeling entitled makes dull tasks drag on. *Personality and Social Psychology Bulletin* 37: 1287-1296.

78 **Entitlement:** Entitlement is often defined as the sense of being owed or deserving certain rights, experiences, or rewards without having earned or meriting them. This perspective leads to an inflated, narcissistic view of one's self as overly important. Another view of entitlement, one that is even more common, is the excessive attachment of feelings to expectations and getting one's own way.

78 **Entitlement messages were delivered subliminally:** As an aside, the response of research participants to entitlement words, even those delivered subliminally, has fascinating implications for society at large. Advertisers make use of entitlement words constantly and most users of media are entitlement-primed with thousands of such messages daily. I wonder about the potential effects of such entitlement-

priming every time I encounter an impatient motorist.

79 **Researchers asked:** S. E. DeVoe and Pfeffer, J. 2011. Time Is Tight: How higher economic value of time increases feelings of time pressure. *Journal of Applied Psychology* 96: 665-676.

80 **The Mommy Track:** While this phrase is also used in business circles, it has a slightly different meaning in academia. In contrast to the career path of so-called serious scholars and researchers, women on the Mommy Track have, at the risk of appearing to not be among their more ambitious peers, dared to reproduce. Academic women on the Mommy Track are, therefore, assumed to be less likely to thrive in tenure track jobs. Indeed, this seems to be borne out by the data in the sense that women are much less likely than men are to rise through the faculty ranks. While the article is a bit old, the very clever pictures drawn by Mary Ann Mason and Marc Goulden in their article, *Do babies matter? The effect of family formation on the lifelong careers of academic men and women,* haven't changed much since the paper was published. (See M. A. Mason and Goulden, M. 2002. *Academe* 88: 21-27 Available online: http://www.aas.org/cswa/status/2004/JANUARY2004/DoBabiesMatter.html). Women who have children later in their academic careers are more successful at attaining tenure but they are not as likely to be promoted beyond the associate level (and, on average, they are also paid less than men of the same rank). See M. West and Curtis, J.W. 2006 AAUP *Faculty Gender Equity Indicators* 2006.

American Association of University Professors.

80 **Scarcity:** My thinking on the topic of scarcity was strongly influenced by Lynne Twist's book, *The Soul of Money.*

81 **Hustle for worthiness:** Brené Brown coined this phrase in *The Gifts of Imperfection* to describe the struggle people encounter as they attempt to earn their sense of personal worth.

82 **Poet David Whyte explains:** The quote was transcribed from David Whyte's audiobook, *What to Remember When Waking: The Disciplines of an Everyday Life* (Sounds True, 2010), Chapter 2, beginning at time 9:57.

I Have Enough Time Now: An Apprenticeship to Enough

88 **Alice:** Name changed to protect privacy.

91 **The War of Art:** Pressfield's book, *The War of Art: Break Through the Blocks and Win Your Creative Battles* (2002, Warner Books), is your best resource on identifying and overcoming resistance. This quote is found on p 12.

91 **Pressfield believes:** If you are still searching for your love(s), take note! What are you resisting the most? Your calling might be hiding behind this fog of resistance.

91 **Brief Daily Session:** I originally found this technique in psychologist Robert Boice's book, *How Writers Journey to*

Comfort and Fluency: A Psychological Adventure (Praeger, 1994).

92 **Margaret:** Real name; used with permission.

96 **Every moment:** Ruth Burrows, OCD. *Essence of Prayer* (Paulist Press, 2006), location 717 in Kindle version.

96 **A short devotional prayer:** I used a prayer to Our Lady UnDoer of Knots and asked Mary to kindly untie the knot of my book. You can find an entire novena (a nine days' prayer) here: http://catholicism.about.com/od/To-Mary-Undoer-of-Knots/qt/Prayer-to- Mary-Undoer-of-Knots.htm.

98 **But when Susan began:** This story was drawn from an interview I conducted with Susan Straight. See An Interview with Novelist Susan Straight published Jan 3, 2007: http://tararobinson.com/blog/2007/01/an_interview_wi.html

101 **A friend of mine:** This story was related to me under conditions of anonymity with permission to use here.

104 **Pomodoro technique:** You can learn much more about the Pomodoro Technique by visiting http://pomodorotechnique.com/

104 **Timer app:** I use FocusTime. You can learn more about it here: http:// focustimeapp.com/

Time Is What I Think It Is: An Apprenticeship to Ease

108   **While it is certainly true:** This statement isn't completely accurate. Gravity affects time, but we don't have access to the kind of technology that takes advantage of those effects—yet.

109   **There's a kind of misperception:** David Whyte audiobook, *What to Remember When Waking.*

111   **When the brain captures more detailed information:** C. Stetson, Fiesta, M.P., and Eagleman, D.M. 2007. Does time really slow down during frightening event? *PLOS One* 2:e1295.

112   **Physiologically:** H. Mori, et al. 2005. How does deep breathing affect office blood pressure and pulse rate? *Hypertension Research* 28: 499-504.

113   **Every breath can be a doorway:** D.G. Benner. *Spirituality and the Awakening Self: The Sacred Journey of Transformation.* (Brazos Press; 2012). Quote is at Location 418 of the Kindle version.

114   **Time is a created thing:** This quote is widely circulated and attributed to Chinese philosopher, Lao Tzu. I have no direct source for it.

114   **The days of thinking of time:** Quote drawn from G. Bilger. 2011. "The Possibilian." *The New Yorker*, April 25, 2011.

115   **Beliefs are mental objects:** Quote is from Alike Jha. "Where belief is born." *The Guardian Online*, published

June 30, 2005, accessed online http:// www.theguardian. com/science/2005/jun/30/psychology.neuroscience

117   **Brené Brown's mantra:** Brown, *Gifts of Imperfection,* Kindle loc 996.

123   **Flow is a mental state:** Definition drawn from http:// en.wikipedia.org/wiki/Flow_ %28psychology%29

123   **No matter how high:** St. Teresa of Avila. *The Interior Castle.* M. Starr, trans. (Riverhead Books, 2003) Quote is drawn from passages on p 45 and p 47.

125   **A recent study:** T.D. Wilson, et al. 2014. Just think: The challenges of the disengaged mind. *Science* 345: 75-77.

125   **Suddenly, the extra minutes were gone:** This is the negative side of flow. Flow can be a positive experience when you intend to lose yourself. But if you're entering flow less intentionally, you can find yourself in a pinch.

125   **Some psychologists believe:** Mind wandering is thought to enhance creativity and problem solving (see Benjamin Baird, et al. 2012. Inspired by distraction: Mind wandering facilitates creative incubation. *Psychological Science* 23: 1117-1122). In addition, the wandering mind activates a suite of brain processing areas collectively known as the "default mode network" which is thought to be important in enhancing social understanding, including empathy (see Wanqing Li, X. Mai, and C. Liu. 2014. The default mode network and

social understanding of others: what do brain connectivity studies tell us. *Frontiers in Human Neuroscience* 8:74).

125 **There is something in every one of you:** Quotes drawn from Howard Thurman. 1980. *The Sound of the Genuine.* Baccalaureate Address – Spelman College, May 4, 1980. Accessed online http://www.ptev.org/hints.aspx?iid=4

All Time Is Precious: An Apprenticeship to Equanimity

133 **Experience is just passing scenery:** This view is attributed to Uchiyama-roshi from his book, *Opening the Hand of Thought,* in Darlene Cohen's article "The Scenery of Cancer," *Shambala Sun,* July 2007. Accessed online: http://www.darlenecohen.net/ welcome/scenery_of_cancer.html

133 **While some may think:** Quote from "Equanimity," adapted from a talk by Gil Fronsdal, May 29, 2004. http://www.insightmeditationcenter.org/books-articles/articles/equanimity/

136 **Mogilner and her colleagues:** Cassie Mogilner, Chance, Z., and Norton, M.I. 2012. Giving time gives you time. *Psychological Science* 23: 1233-1238.

137 **Having done this research:** Quote drawn from interview with Cassie Mogilner which aired on Radio Boston on April 23, 2012, accessed online at http://radioboston.wbur.org/2012/04/23/giving-time. Quote is at 22:12 in the interview.

138 **In an act of giving:** Quotes drawn from Sharon Salzberg. 2014. "Generosity's Perfection." Accessed online http://www.sharonsalzberg.com/generositys-perfection/

141 **When you insist:** This story and quotes are drawn from Darlene Cohen, "The Scenery of Cancer," *Shambala Sun,* July 2007.

142 **If you always go with your preference:** Ibid.

143 **A relaxed decision:** Quoted in David G. Benner. *Desiring God's Will: Aligning Our Hearts with the Heart of God* (IVP Books, 2009) Kindle Loc 136.

144 **A spirit of willingness:** Benner, *Desiring God's Will,* loc 167

144 **A life or preference:** Cohen, "The Scenery of Cancer."

147 **Human brains tend to discount:** For a review of the science behind temporal discounting of rewards, see Gregory S. Berns, Laibson, D., and Loewenstein, G. 2007. Intertemporal choice — toward an integrative framework. *Trends in Cognitive Sciences* 11: 482-488.

147 **In experiments aimed at understanding:** David DeSteno, et al. 2014. Gratitude: A tool for reducing economic impatience. *Psychological Science* 25: 1262-1267.

147 **Grateful folks were far more likely:** Monica Y. Bartlett and DeSteno, D. 2006. Gratitude and prosocial behavior: Helping when it costs you. *Psychological Science* 17: 319-325.

147   **Embrace the gratitude:** Quote was drawn from David DeSteno, "Gratitude is about the future, not the past," *The Huffington Post* published on Sept. 21, 2013. http://www.huffingtonpost.com/david-desteno/gratitude-research_b_3932043.html

Putting Love Into Action

151   **I once asked a bird:** I used this quote at the beginning of my dissertation because it described how I managed to keep going through the darkest times of my graduate career. Hafiz. "She Responded." David Ladinsky, translator. *The Gift: Poems of Hafiz the Great Sufi Master.* (Penguin Compass; 1999).

Setting Direction with Discernment

163   **Online inventory:** I recommend the VIA Survey of Character Strengths as a great place to start. The twenty-four character strengths were identified by leading psychologists in the field of Positive Psychology and are common to all human beings. Other strengths tests, such as StrengthsFinder 2.0, tend to be proprietary and jargon based, while the VIA is easier to understand and to apply to one's life. To access the VIA Survey of Character Strengths, visit https://www.authentichappiness.sas.upenn.edu/ and follow the link to Questionnaires.

165   **Discernment is best undertaken:** According to some authors, receiving the results of discernment is a very significant matter. To learn what that your direction could be and to know what you are being invited to do, and then refuse those, means potentially risking the fulfillment of your life. See Alfred Delp, S.J. *Advent of the Heart: Seasonal Sermons and Prison Writings 1941-1944* (Ignatius Press; 2006), Kindle loc 803 - 812.

165   **You will never be lead:** Sincere discernment includes discarding options that are morally wrong and those that are clearly harmful to others. If you're concerned or you want guidance in the discernment process, seek the help of a trained spiritual director who is familiar with Ignatian discernment.

165   **An ancient method of decision-making:** St. Ignatius of Loyola created a systematic process for decision-making based on using one's emotions as a means of understanding divine intentions. You can learn more about Ignatian decision-making by visiting http://www.ignatianspirituality. com/making-good-decisions/

168   **Predicting which choices will bring satisfaction:** The science of "affective forecasting" is devoted to understanding how well people can predict which choices will bring them the greatest happiness. Indications are that people usually guess wrong when trying to decide what option will yield

the best result. See Brett Pelham. 2004. Affective forecasting: The perils of predicting future feelings. *Psychological Science Agenda* published online April 2004. http://www.apa.org/science/about/psa/2004/04/ pelham.aspx

169   **When Amy and I met:** Name and story used with permission.

Taking Vision Into Action With a Heart- Centered Plan

177   **Camino de Santiago de Compostela:** The "Camino" is a tradition pilgrimage route beginning in France and ending 500 miles later in Spain.

180   **Getting Things Done:** If you don't already have a strong task management background, this might be a good time to explore getting one. Despite many of its flaws (mentioned in the Introduction of this book), I continue to recommend David Allen's *Getting Things Done* methodology for task management as a best practice.

Keeping Your Promises to Yourself

186   **Divine love meets us:** Burrows, *Essence of Prayer,* Kindle loc 721.

190   **When the enemy of human nature:** St. Ignatius of Loyola. *The Spiritual Exercises of St. Ignatius of Loyola.* Fr. Elder Mullan, S.J., Translator. (P.J. Kenedy and Sons, 1914

[Original publication date 1548]), accessed online http://www.ccel.org/ccel/ignatius/exercises.xix.i.html. From the 13th Rule in the first week.

190   **Augusto:** His real name, used with permission.

192   **The traditional prayer form:** You can learn more about the Daily Examen by visiting http://www.ignatianspirituality.com/ignatian-prayer/the-examen/

192   **The steps for undertaking:** The form of Examen presented here is loosely based on the process suggested by Father Timothy Gallagher in his book, *The Examen Prayer: Ignatian Wisdom for Our Lives Today* (Crossroad Publishing Company; 2006).

Receiving Results with Grace

196   **Whatever goodness or virtue is in you:** Thomas à Kempis. *The Imitation of Christ* C.L. Fitzpatrick, editor. (Catholic Book Publishing Corp., 1993 [original publication date ca. 1418]); quote is from Kindle loc 335.

196   **This human being is a guest house:** "The Guest House" by Jelaluddin Rumi, translated by Coleman Barks. Accessed online at http://www.pbs.org/wnet/foolingwithwords/Pbarks_poem10.html

197   **Simple Abundance:** Sarah Ban Breathnach. *Simple Abundance: A Daybook of Comfort and Joy.* (Grand Central

Publishing, 2008).

197 **Sunlight is what changes:** Quote was drawn from "Barbara Fredrickson: Positive Emotions Open Our Mind," YouTube video: https://www.youtube.com/watch?v=Z7dFDHzV36g#t=141

198 **Lasting cognitive resource:** Barbara Fredrickson. 2001. The role of positive emotions in positive psychology: The broaden-and-build- theory of positive emotions. *American Psychologist* 56: 218-226.

199 **Three Good Things Exercise:** Martin Seligman, et al. 2005. Positive psychology progress: Empirical validation of interventions. *American Psychologist* 60: 410-421.

199 **Kristin:** Name changed to protect privacy; story used with permission.

200 **Women are poor negotiators:** Alice F. Stuhlmacher and Walters, A.E. 1999. Gender differences in negotiation outcome: A meta-analysis. *Personnel Psychology* 52: 653-677.

203 **The throes of desolation:** Desolation is a spiritual condition distinct from depression, which is an emotional (and usually neurochemical) state. St. Ignatius of Loyola described desolation as a "darkness of the soul...which lead(s) to a loss of faith." See Fr. Andrew B. Garcia, S.J. 2011. Learning from desolation. *New Jesuit Review* 2. Accessed online: http://www.newjesuitreview.org/newjesuitreview/ Vol._2,_

Notes

No._7,_A._1.html

203   **No precipitating cause:** Unlike sadness or depression,
which has a context in life such as the death of a loved one,
desolation often occurs without a precipitating cause. In
other words, discouragement and loss of hope seems to
appear "out of nowhere."

204   **Dark night of the soul:** The poem, "The Dark Night of
the Soul," was written by St. John of the Cross in 1578 and
describes the hardships and difficulties of the soul's journey
to God. Subsequently, the phrase has been used in spiritual
circles to describe periods of prolonged dryness, desolation,
and spiritual adversity.

CPSIA information can be obtained at www.ICGtesting.com
Printed in the USA
BVOW02s2036160316

440607BV00002B/3/P